Elementary Music Rudiments© 2023 by San Marco Publications. All rights reserved.

All right reserved. No part of this book may be reproduced in any form or by electronic or mechanical means including Information storage and retrieval systems without permission in writing from the author.

ISBN: 1-896499-50-3

Contents

Level 1	2
Level 2	10
Level 3	13
Level 4	19
Level 5	29
Level 6	41
Level 7	50
Level 8	67

History Level 1

The Orchestra

An *orchestra* is a performing group made up of many different musical instruments. Orchestra is a Greek word that originally referred to the area directly in front of a stage. When you attend an orchestral performance, you will see the orchestra playing in that exact place.

The orchestra as we know it today began with Italian opera around the year 1600. Opera was a sung play composed for singers and accompanied by a group of musicians that sat in front of the stage. Early orchestras performed short pieces called *overtures* before the opera started.

The music produced by these groups became so popular that composers started to write large pieces exclusively for them called *symphonies*. This is the reason orchestras are often called 'symphony orchestras.'

By the middle of the 19th century, these orchestras developed a standard group of instruments that has remained to the present day. The modern orchestra contains four main instrument sections:

- **strings** (violin, viola, cello, bass)
- **woodwinds** (flute, clarinet, oboe, bassoon, piccolo, English horn)
- **brass** (trumpet, trombone, tuba, French horn)
- **percussion** (timpani, drums, triangle, gong, cymbals, xylophone, piano, tambourine, +)

To keep the orchestra together, and help them play with the correct rhythm and expression, a *conductor* stands in front of them and directs them using hand gestures.

Camille Saint-Saens (1835 - 1921) Romantic Era

Camille Saint-Saens was born October 9, 1835, in Paris, France. He began studying piano at age two and a half and wrote his first piano piece when he was three. He started performing when he was a young boy and made his Paris recital debut at the age of ten.

Saint-Saens was not just brilliant at music. He also excelled at mathematics and science. He studied music at the Paris Conservatoire and won many prizes there. He became a follower of the great virtuoso pianist, organist, and composer, Franz Liszt.

Saint-Saens composed almost every kind of musical work including symphonies, concertos, and operas. One of his compositions, the Carnival of the Animals, was written as a sort of joke, but it is now his most famous work. He also wrote, books, poetry, and plays.

Saint-Saens influenced other well know French composers, especially Maurice Ravel and Gabriel Fauré.

Saint-Saens is considered a Romantic composer. The Romantic era was a period in time from approximately 1820 to 1910. There are many great composers from this era including:

- Frédéric Chopin
- Robert Schumann
- Felix Mendelssohn
- Johannes Brahms
- Pyotr Tchaikovsky
- Franz Liszt
- Hector Berlioz

The Carnival of the Animals

One of Saint-Saens most well-known compositions is **The Carnival of the Animals**. It is written for two pianos and orchestra. He had fun describing some of his friends as animals. This piece is known throughout the world for its musical portrayal of animals. Some of the animals he portrays in music include the lion, hens and roosters, the turtle, the elephant, the kangaroo, the cuckoo, and the swan. There are also sections describing an aquarium, an aviary, fossils, people with long ears (donkeys), and a pianist. We will discuss the pieces titled: *Kangaroos, Aquarium,* and *The Swan*. The Carnival of the Animals is *descriptive* or **program music**. Program music is designed to portray a picture, object or story with sound.

Kangaroos
Saint-Saens wrote *Kangaroos* for two pianos. The main melody features hopping 5ths in the theme. When they go up, the tempo gradually speeds up, and the dynamics get louder. When the fifths go down, the tempo gradually slows down, and the dynamics get quieter.

Aquarium
Aquarium is written for two pianos, strings, flute and glass harmonica. In this piece, the composer describes water by trickling runs on the two pianos. The swimming of the fish is portrayed by a smooth melody in the strings and flute. The sound of water droplets was written for the **glass harmonica**, an instrument from the 19th century. It produces a sound much like when you run your fingers around the top of a water glass. It is usually played on the glockenspiel today because glass harmonicas are difficult to find.

The Swan
The Swan is the most famous section of The Carnival of the Animals. It is written for two pianos and cello. A beautiful melody is played by the cello while the pianos play rippling notes and broken chords that describe the swans feet gliding under the water.

Search the internet and listen to a performance of Carnival of the Animals.

Camille Saint Saens Crossword

Complete the crossword below.

Word List

Swan
Two
Turtle
Romantic
Elephant
Orchestra
Kangaroo
France
Cello
Donkey
Hens
Glass Harmonica
Two Pianos

Across

3. Chickens
4. Long eared animal
6. Where Saint Saens was born
7. Carnival of the Animals is written for 2 pianos and _____
12. Era in which Saint Saens composed
13. Number of pianos in Carnival of the Animals

Down

1. The Swan is written for _____
2. Rare instrument used in Aquarium
5. Jumping Australian animal
8. Large African animal with trunk
9. Instruments featured in Kangaroos
10. Slow moving animal with shell
11. Gliding water bird

Choose the correct answer.

a. An orchestra is led by the:	☐	Pitcher	☐	Conductor
	☐	President	☐	Mayor

b. This instrument is not part of the string section	☐	Violin	☐	Cello
	☐	Viola	☐	Maracas

c. This instrument is not part of the woodwind section:	☐	Flute	☐	Oboe
	☐	Clarinet	☐	French Horn

d. Camille Saint-Saens was born in:	☐	Canada	☐	France
	☐	China	☐	Russia

e. Saint-Saens wrote his first piano piece when he was:	☐	3	☐	2
	☐	10	☐	32

f. Carnival of the Animals is written for orchestra and:	☐	Flute	☐	2 pianos
	☐	3 banjos	☐	Trumpet

g. This animal is not in Carnival of the Animals:	☐	Kangaroo	☐	Elephant
	☐	Wolf	☐	Lion

h. Aquarium is written for 2 pianos, strings, flute, and:	☐	Cello	☐	Horn
	☐	Guitar	☐	Glass Harmonica

i. The Swan is written for 2 pianos and:	☐	Flute	☐	Cello
	☐	Lute	☐	Harp

j. Carnival of the Animals is:	☐	Rock Music	☐	Program Music
	☐	Jazz Music	☐	Opera

Sergei Prokofiev (1891 - 1953) Modern Era

Russian composer and pianist **Sergei Prokofiev** was born in 1891 in a small village in Ukraine. From a young age, he had a gift for music. Prokofiev began studying piano with his mother when he was three. At five, he wrote his first composition, and at nine, he wrote his first opera. He studied music at the St Petersburg Conservatory from 1904 to 1914.

Prokofiev was a gifted pianist and often performed his works in concert.

Prokofiev's music was more innovative and different sounding than anything ever heard before. It used unusual harmonies and intense rhythms.

After the Russian revolution, Prokofiev moved to America. However, American audiences did not fully appreciate his music. In 1923 he settled in Paris where he was very successful, and his music was well received. In 1936 Prokofiev returned to Russia, where he spent the last 19 years of his life. During this period, he wrote some of his best works.

Prokofiev loved to use music to tell a story. One of his most famous compositions that tells a story is **Peter and the Wolf,** which he composed for Russia's Central Children's Theatre. In addition to symphonies, Prokofiev wrote ballets, operas, concertos, piano pieces, movie scores and more.

Peter and the Wolf

Prokofiev wrote Peter and the Wolf in 1936 for narrator and orchestra. It is a story in music that includes both people and animals.
Like Saint-Saens Carnival of the Animals, this is program music. Here, along with a narrator, the music tells a story.

Each character in the story has a particular instrument and a musical theme:

- Peter: string instruments (including violin, viola, cello, and bass)
- Bird: flute
- Cat: clarinet
- Duck: oboe
- Grandfather: bassoon
- Hunters: woodwind theme, with gunshots on timpani and bass drum
- Wolf: French horns

Peter, a young boy, lives with his grandfather near a forest. One day, Peter goes out, leaving the garden gate open, and the duck that lives in the yard gets out and goes swimming in a nearby pond. The duck starts arguing with a little bird. Peter's pet cat sneaks up on them quietly, and the bird flies to safety in a tall tree while the duck swims to the middle of the pond.

Peter's grandfather is angry at him for being in the forest alone. What if a wolf was in the forest? Peter says: "Boys like me are not afraid of wolves." His grandfather takes him back into the house. Afterword, "a big, grey wolf" does come out of the forest. The cat climbs into a tree, but the duck, who has jumped out of the pond, is caught and swallowed by the wolf.

Peter grabs a rope and scampers over the garden wall into the tree. He tells the bird to fly around the wolf's head and distract it. Then he catches the wolf by the tail.

Hunters come out of the forest and want to shoot the wolf, but Peter convinces them to take the wolf to a zoo. The narrator completes the story by saying: "If you listen very carefully, you'll hear the duck quacking inside the wolf's belly because the wolf in his hurry had swallowed her alive."

Search the internet and listen to a performance of Peter and the Wolf.

Sergei Prokofiev Word Search

```
S T R I N G S D Q O
R E F I V E V C D R
P R O G R A M L U C
J U T Y U I O P C H
H S X C W O L F K E
G S A M O D E R N S
F I B A S S O O N T
D A G O A D C N M R
B I R D G H A E R A
O B O E A T T B E D
```

Word List

Russia
wolf
oboe
five
duck
bassoon
Modern
program
cat
orchestra
bird
strings

1. Where was Prokofiev born? _____

2. At what age did Prokofiev begin composing? _____

3. In what musical era did he compose? _____

4. Peter and the Wolf is written for narrator and _____

5. What type of music is Peter and the Wolf? _____

6. Name 4 animals in Peter and the Wolf. _____ _____ _____ _____

7. What instruments are used to portray Peter? _____

8. What instrument is used to portray the grandfather? _____

9. What instument is used to portray the duck? _____

9

History Level 2

Wolfgang Amadeus Mozart (1756 - 1791) Classical Era

Wolfgang Amadeus Mozart composed music in the ***classical era.*** The classical era was a period in history between the years 1730 and 1820. Mozart was born in Salzburg, Austria, where his father and teacher Leopold was a violinist and composer. Wolfgang was a child prodigy. He composed his first piece of music at age five, had his first piece published when he was seven, and he wrote his first opera when he was twelve. By the time Mozart was 6, he was a first-rate pianist and violinist. He and his sister Maria Anna (known as Nannerl) traveled all over Europe performing for royalty.

As an adult, Mozart moved to Vienna, to work as a pianist and composer. Mozart, no longer a child prodigy, was still a musical genius, but people no longer made a big fuss over him. At that time, musicians were treated like servants, but Mozart could never and would never think of himself as a servant.

Mozart was only 35 when he died. During his short life, he composed in all different musical forms, including operas, symphonies, concertos, masses, and chamber music. Today, he is still considered one of the greatest composers of all time!

Catalogue Numbers for Mozart Compositions

Many composers assigned numbers to their compositions. This helped to identify them. If a composer wrote four Sonatas in C major, it was easier to identify them if they were numbered. Mozart, however, never numbered his works.

In 1862, a Viennese botanist and teacher named Ludwig von Köchel, published a catalogue of Mozart's compositions in chronological order. He assigned Köchel (K) numbers to each of Mozarts works according to the date of composition. For example, the Horn Concerto we are going to study is labeled K495. It is approximately the 495th piece of music that Mozart composed.

Horn Concerto No. 4 in E flat Major, K 495

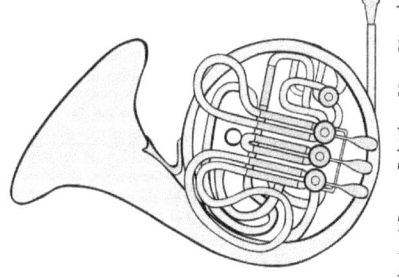

A ***concerto*** is a musical composition which features a single solo instrumentalist with an orchestral accompaniment. It shows off the skills of the soloist and the musical potential of the instrument being played.

This concerto is for french horn and orchestra. It was written my Mozart in 1786 for his friend, French horn player, Joseph Leutgeb.

Mozart wrote it in four colors of ink, black, red, blue, and green as a joke for his friend Joseph. Mozart had a great sense of humor.

This concerto has four sections called ***movements***.

The last movement is a ***Rondo***. It features a melody which is a hunting theme, which returns over and over throughout the piece. Rondos always have a section that returns many times over. Between this section are new sections consisting of different melodies or themes and musical ideas. After each new idea the original theme returns. Find and listen to a recording of this Rondo on the internet.

Twelve Variations on "Ah vous dirai-je, Maman"

Twelve Variations on "Ah vous dirai-je, Maman" K. 265, is a piano composition by Mozart, composed when he was about 25 years old (1781 or 1782). In music, variations are pieces that are based on a tune, known as the theme. This form is often called Theme and Variations. This piece consists of twelve variations on the French folk song "Ah! vous dirai-je, Maman". This well-known melody first appeared in 1761, and has been used for many children's songs, such as "Twinkle Twinkle Little Star," "Baa, Baa, Black Sheep," and the "Alphabet Song."

Mozart's Variations are composed for solo piano and consist of 13 sections; the first section is the theme, the other sections are Variations 1 to 12.

The variations were first published in Vienna in 1785.

Choose the correct answer.

a. Mozart was born in:	☐	France	☐	Germany
	☐	Poland	☐	Austria

b. Mozart's first teacher was:	☐	His father	☐	His mother
	☐	His sister	☐	Haydn

c. What era did Mozart live?	☐	modern	☐	classical
	☐	romantic	☐	baroque

d. What is the solo instrument in Mozart's Horn concerto?	☐	flute	☐	piano
	☐	french horn	☐	oboe

e. Mozart's Horn Concerto in E♭ has 4 sections called:	☐	groups	☐	movements
	☐	pieces	☐	dances

f. The last movement of Mozart's Horn Concerto in E♭ is a:	☐	rondo	☐	waltz
	☐	sonata	☐	minuet

g. Mozart's Variations on Ah vous dirai-je, Maman are written for:	☐	guitar	☐	orchestra
	☐	piano	☐	horn

h. How many variations did Mozart write on Ah vous dirai-je Maman?	☐	12	☐	9
	☐	6	☐	32

i. The melody upon which variations are based is called the:	☐	subject	☐	phrase
	☐	tune	☐	theme

j. The melody of these variations has been used for these childrens songs:	☐	Twinkle Twinkle	☐	Baa Baa Black Sheep
	☐	Alphabet Song	☐	Mary Had a Little Lamb

History Level 3

Johann Sebastian Bach (1685 - 1750) Baroque Era

Johann Sebastian Bach was born in Eisenach, Germany where his father, a musician, taught him to play violin and harpsichord. Many of Bach's relatives were also musicians. His older brother, Johann Christoph Bach taught him to play the organ.

In 1707, Bach married his cousin Maria Barbara Bach. They had seven children. Maria died, and Bach married Anna Magdalena Wilcke in 1721. They had 13 more children. In total, Bach had 20 children. Some of Bach's sons became well-known composers. Carl Phillip Emmanuel Bach and Johann Christian Bach are two of them.

One of Bach's first serious jobs was working for a duke. After that, he was hired to compose for a prince. His final job was the director of music at St. Thomas Church and School in Leipzig, Germany. Here he was cantor (music teacher), organist, and music composer. He was very busy teaching, conducting, performing, and writing music. While in Leipzig he conducted a small group of local musicians who sometimes played at coffee houses.

Bach wrote a lot of music. His works fill many large volumes and contain, choral music, concertos, orchestra and chamber music and organ and keyboard music. Some of Bachs most famous compositions are the Brandenburg Concertos and The Well Tempered Clavier, written as teaching pieces for his students. He also wrote many great works for organ including the famous Toccata and Fugue in D minor.

Bach is considered one of the greatest musicians and composers that ever lived. However, during his life, he was hardly known. About 100 years after his death another composer named Felix Mendelssohn brought attention to his music, and the world finally realized Bach's greatness.

Bach composed during the Baroque era, which was between the years 1600 and 1750. Baroque music has tuneful melodies and can be very dramatic. The melodies are often very elaborate and decorated with trills and ornaments. Bach died in 1750.

The Anna Magdalena Bach Notebook

The *Anna Magdalena Bach Notebook* refers to two books that composer Johann Sebastian Bach gave to his second wife, Anna Magdalena on her birthday. Bach wanted Anna Magdalena to copy music of her choosing into the books. They contain keyboard music and a few pieces for voice.

One book is dated 1722, and the other is dated 1725. The better-known book is the one from 1725. It is richly decorated with gold leaf and is a beautiful book.

Anna Magdalena was a musician and singer. Most of the pieces in the book are in Anna Magdalena's handwriting, and the true identity of many of the original composers in the book is not known. There seems to be writing in the book by members of Bach's family including Carl Phillip Emmanuel Bach, and Johann Christian Bach, two of his sons. The first two pieces in the book were copied by J. S. Bach himself.

The books contain several dances, arias, chorales and other pieces of music by different composers. These composers were probably Carl Philip Emmanuel Bach, Christian Petzold, François Couperin, and other musician friends of the Bach family.

Most of these pieces were written for musical enjoyment, but also as teaching pieces for younger members of the Bach family.

Anna Magdalena loved to have musical gatherings at the Bach house where visitors were encouraged to perform and compose new pieces which were copied into the notebook.

The Harpischord

The **harpsichord,** a keyboard instrument, is an early relative of the piano. It looks a little like a grand piano but sounds much different.
The harpsichord has small hooks called quills that pluck the string when a player presses a key on the keyboard. Because of this, it is very challenging to make dynamic changes when playing the harpsichord. Since the strings are plucked, the keyboard is not touch sensitive, and the player does not have control over the volume of each note.
The pieces in the Anna Magdalena Notebook were written for a harpsichord or a similar keyboard instrument.

The Baroque Dance

A *Baroque dance* is an instrumental dance composed during the Baroque era (1600 - 1750). Dance music was very popular in the Baroque era, and composers were often asked to write dances for parties and functions.

The Anna Magdalena Notebook contains some of these Baroque dances written for keyboard. One of the most common dances found in this notebook is the *minuet*. A minuet is a dance for two people in 3/4 time that originated in France. It may be spelled differently in different countries. In Italy, it was called the *minuetto* and in France the *menuet*. Eventually, minuets were written for non-dancing purposes and became a musical form used for keyboard pieces and movements of symphonies. Minuets can also be found in operas, ballets, and plays.

One of the most famous minuets ever written, the *Minuet in G Major*, is in the Anna Magdalena Notebook. We are not exactly sure who wrote it, but credit is given to the composer Christian Petzold. The melody from this minuet has been used in pop songs and movie themes. The example below contains the opening eight measures of this famous minuet. Play it and see if you recognize it.

Another common dance from the Baroque era is the ***gavotte***. The gavotte is a folk dance from France. The music for a gavotte has a four beat feel and is moderately fast. It usually starts with upbeats (or an anacrusis) on beats three and four. Gavottes written in the Baroque period were not written for dancing but as musical pieces to listen to and enjoy.

Composers began writing ***Suites***, which were larger compositions consisting of six or seven short dance-based pieces. The gavotte was often one of these pieces. The best-known examples of the gavotte are found in the suites written by J.S.Bach.

The following musical excerpt is the beginning of the Gavotte from J.S. Bach's French Suite in G major, BWV 816. BWV is a catalog number given to Bach's compositions to identify them. This gavotte is the fourth dance in the suite, and it is written for harpsichord.

This dance begins with two quarter note upbeats. This is a characteristic of a gavotte. The time signature ₵ is an abbreviation for 2/2 time. The top number tells us that there are two beats in each measure and the bottom number tells us that the half note receives one beat.

In this piece, the stems in the treble clef are placed in two directions. This indicates that the right hand is playing two different melodies. One melody has the stems going up, and one melody has the stems going down. The lower melody in the treble clef in mm.3-4 has three quarter rests. Here, the bottom voice is resting. The bass clef has its own melody. Music from the Baroque period is often based on 2, 3, 4, or more melodies that all work together to create a composition. This is called ***counterpoint***.

Search the internet for a recording of this Gavotte. Try to find a performance using the harpsichord to hear how it sounds on this instrument.

Another popular dance in the Baroque suite is the *gigue*. Gigue is the French word for a lively dance in triple time. In Italian, it is called "*giga*," and in English, it is "*jig*." The gigue is often seen in the Baroque dance suite as the last piece or movement.

Gigues use time signatures like 6/8, 9/8, or 12/16. Melodies are made up of rapidly moving groups of three eighth or three sixteenth notes. Most gigues are divided into four measure phrases and are written in counterpoint, using 2, 3, or more melodies that work together.

The following excerpt is the Gigue from French Suite in G Major, BWV 816, by J.S. Bach. This piece is written for harpsichord. The gigue begins with one melody in the treble clef. A second melody starts at the end of measure 3 in the treble clef. Here, the stems go in the opposite direction to show the two different melodies. A third melody is added at the end of measure 6, in the left hand. All three of these lines work together to create a masterful piece of music.

Answer the following questions.

a) What musical era did J.S. Bach live? _____

b) When did this era occur? _____

c) In what country was he born? _____

d) What is the Anna Magdalena Notebook? _____

e) Name two composers whose music is in the Anna Magdalena Notebook.

    1) _____

    2) _____

f) Name three types of pieces found the the Anna Magdalena Notebook.

    1) _____ 2) _____ 3) _____

g) What instrument are these pieces written for? _____

h) What type of instrument is this? _____

i) In what country did the minuet originate? _____

j) What is the time signature of a minuet? _____

k) In what country did the gavotte originate? _____

l) Does the gavotte begin with an anacrusis? _____

m) What is a suitable Italian term for the tempo of a gigue? _____

n) The notes of a gigue usually occur in groups of _____

o) Where does the gigue usually occur in the Baroque dance suite? _____

History Level 4

The Orchestra

An *orchestra* is a large group of musicians playing various instruments. The orchestra is lead by the *conductor*. It is divided into groups of related instruments called *sections*. The four main sections of the orchestra are:

- Strings
- Woodwinds
- Brass
- Percussion

Strings

String instruments use vibrating strings to make sound. The strings are stretched across the hollow body of the instrument and plucked or played with a bow. The string section consists of:

- Violins
- Violas
- Cellos
- Double basses
- Harp

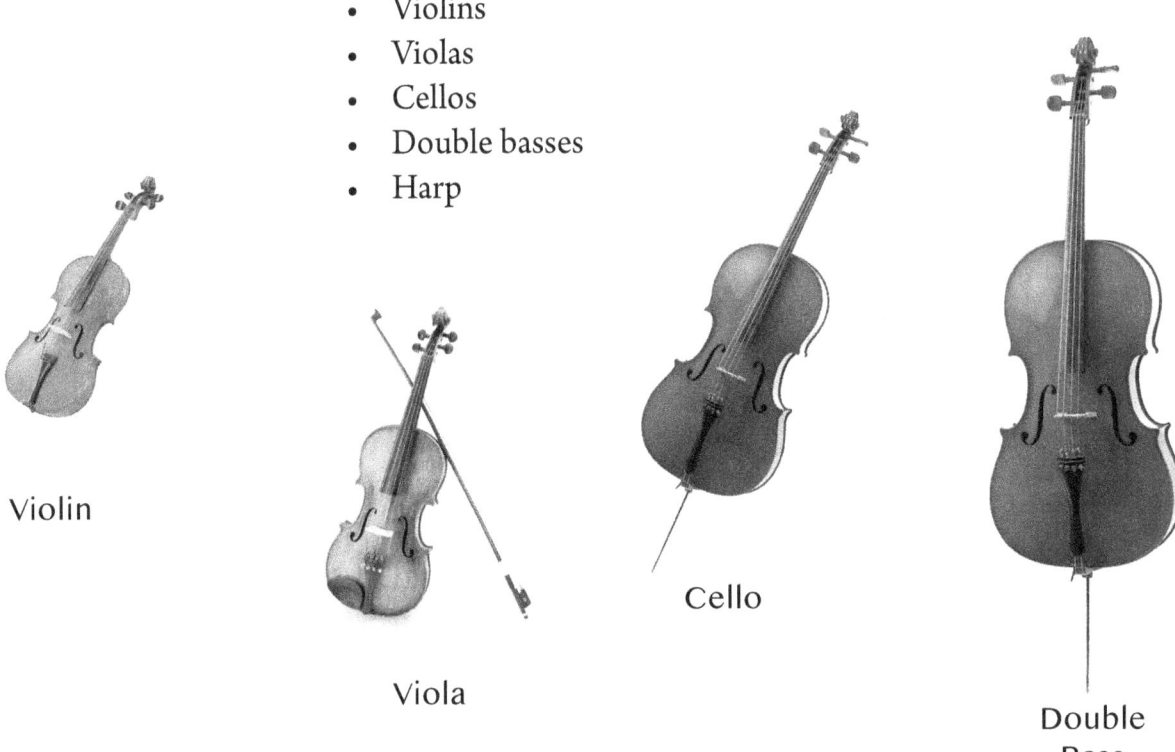

Violin

Viola

Cello

Double Bass

Woodwinds

Woodwind instruments consist of long hollow tubes of wood or metal. The player creates sound by blowing air through a thin piece of shaved wood called a 'reed' or blowing across a mouthpiece. Finger holes on the instruments are open and closed to change the pitch. The woodwind section consists of:

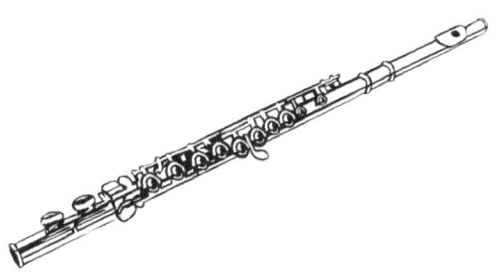

- Clarinets
- Flutes and Piccolos
- Oboes
- Bassoons and Double Bassoons
- Saxophones

Brass

Brass instruments are wind instruments made of metal with a cup-shaped mouthpiece. The player creates sound by pressing his or her lips together in the mouthpiece and pushing air out as if they were making a buzzing sound. This creates a vibrating column of air inside the instrument and produces sound. The brass section is made up of:

- Horns
- Trumpets
- Trombones
- Tubas

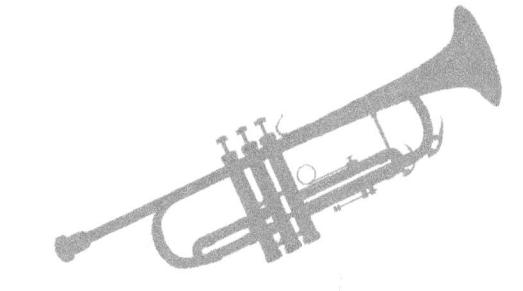

Percussion

Percussion instruments are instruments that are played by being struck or shaken. There are many percussion instruments. Some create specific pitches like the marimba, xylophone, and the timpani. These are some of the instruments of the percussion section:

- Bass drum
- Chimes
- Gong
- Triangle
- Cymbals
- Snare drum

- Tambourine
- Drum
- Timpani
- Xylophone
- Marimba

Figure 4.1 is a standard seating chart for an orchestra.

Figure 4.1

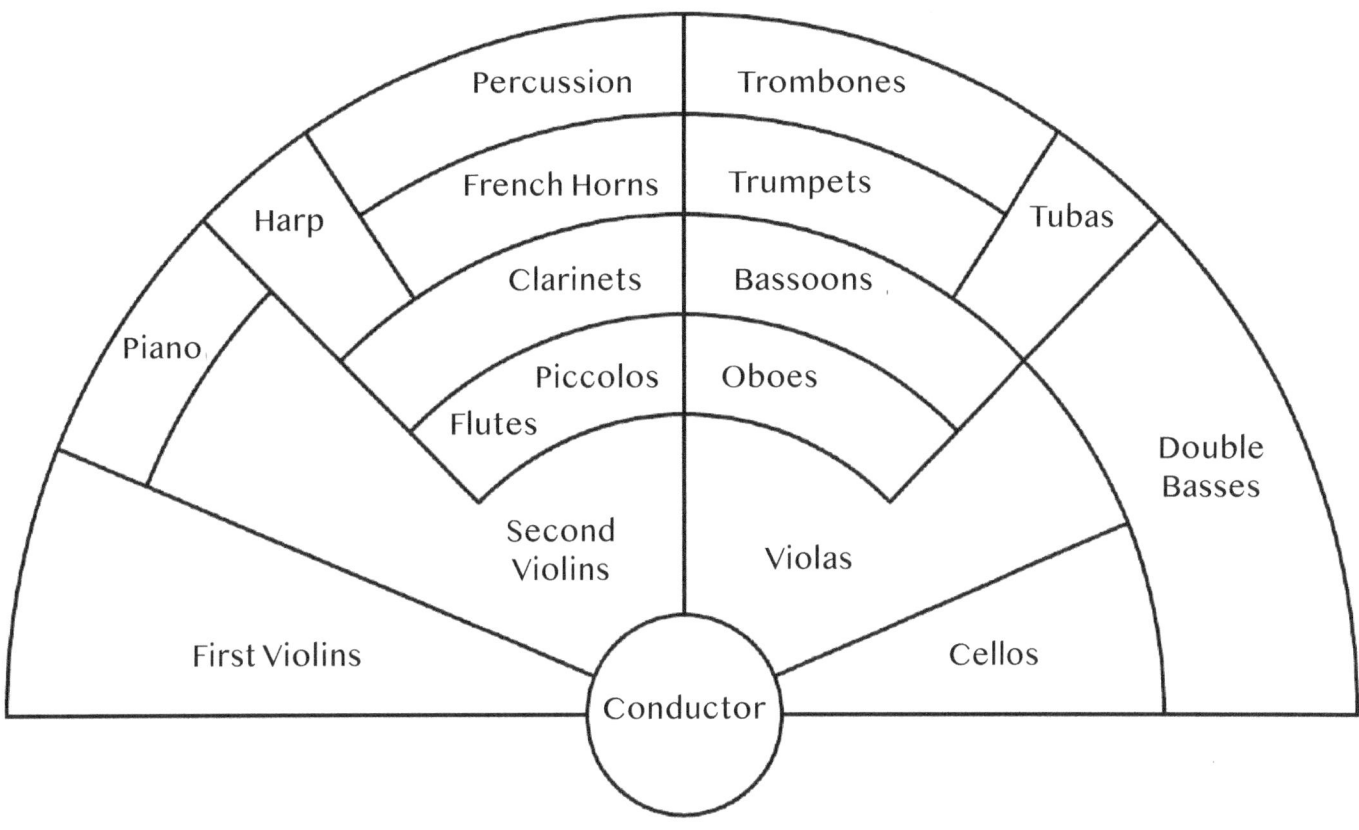

Music Terms

Review the following musical terms from Levels 1 to 4 that are related to style.

cantabile — in a singing style

dolce — sweetly

grazioso — gracefully

maestoso — majestically

marcato — marked or stressed

Benjamin Britten (1913 - 1976) Modern Era

Benjamin Britten was an accomplished conductor, composer, and pianist. He was born in Lowestoft, a town on the English seacoast on November 22nd, the feast day of St. Cecilia, the patron saint of music. Benjamin's mother was a singer and often held concerts in their home.

Britton won a scholarship to the Royal College of Music in London, and his first job was writing music for films.

He did not believe in war and when England decided to go to war with Germany in 1939, Britten left for America. However, he had a great love for the United Kingdom, and in the middle of World War II, he sailed back to his native country.

After the war, the largest opera company in England held a gala and commissioned Britten to write them a new opera. He also composed an opera to honor the coronation of Queen Elizabeth II. Benjamin Britton was the first musician to be gifted with the title of "Lord" by the Queen.

Young Persons Guide to the Orchestra

The **Young Person's Guide to the Orchestra** is a composition for orchestra written in 1946 by Benjamin Britten. It was initially written for an educational film called *Instruments of the Orchestra* featuring the London Symphony Orchestra. It is one of Britten's best-known compositions.

Young Persons Guide to the Orchestra is based on a piece titled *Rondeau* by the Baroque composer Henry Purcell. The form of Britton's composition is *Theme and Variations*. In this form, the theme is stated first, followed by 13 variations. The variations are short pieces based on the theme that vary in mood and sound. Young Persons Guide to the Orchestra is specifically designed to feature the instruments of the orchestra.

The work begins with the theme (based on Purcell's Rondeau) performed by all the instruments of the orchestra. This is followed by each family of instrument: first the woodwinds, then the brass, then the strings, and finally the percussion. Each variation features an instrument in detail and moves through the family from the highest to the lowest sounding. The first variation starts with piccolos and flutes. Following that, each member of the woodwinds gets a variation including the oboes, the clarinets, and finally the lowest sounding bassoons. The variations then go through the strings, the brass, and ends with the percussion.

After the whole orchestra has played through the instrumental sections (13 variations), all of the instruments join together in the final section to perform a fugue* which starts with the piccolo, followed by the woodwinds, strings, brass, and percussion. Once everyone has entered, the brass section is heard again along with a bang on the gong playing Purcell's original melody. Find a recording of Young Persons Guide to the Orchestra on the internet and listen to it.

*A *fugue* is a composition with two or more voices or parts, in which the melody (called the subject), is played by one voice or part and then replayed and changed by the other voices or parts. Fugues contain between two to five parts.

Answer the following questions.

a. Who composed Young Persons Guide to the Orchestra? _____

b. In what country was he born? _____

c. In what era did he live? _____

d. Who composed the theme on which this work is based? _____

e. What era did this composer live? _____

f. How many variations are in Young Persons Guide to the Orchestra? _____

g. What are the four instrument families featured in this composition?

    1. _____

    2. _____

    3. _____

    4. _____

h. What type of piece is the final movement of this composition? _____

Piotr Ilyich Tchaikovsky (1840 - 1893) Romantic Era

Piotr Ilyich Tchaikovsky was born in Votkinsk, a town in Russia's Ural Mountains. His father was a Ukrainian mining engineer. He began piano lessons when he was five years old. In 1850 he moved to the city of St. Petersburg. Here, Tchaikovsky studied law because music was not considered an acceptable profession.

While in law school, Tchaikovsky continued to study music. He attended the opera and theater with his classmates. At age 23 he gave up his legal job with the Ministry of Justice and went to study music full time at the St. Petersburg Conservatory. In 1863, he moved to Moscow, where he became a professor of harmony at the Moscow Conservatory. It is now named after him.

Tchaikovsky wrote six symphonies, the famous Piano Concerto in B♭ major, a handful of operas and three ballets of which, "Swan Lake," "The Nutcracker" and "Sleeping Beauty" are his most famous works. During his life, his music was extremely popular, and he was in great demand as a conductor.

For many years, Tchaikovsky had a patroness named Nadezhda von Meck -- a wealthy widow who supported the arts and artists. She sent him money monthly so that he could concentrate on composing without having to worry about making a living. For 14 years they communicated by letter, but von Meck insisted that they never meet in person. Tchaikovsky dedicated his Fourth Symphony to her.

Tchaikovsky traveled all over Europe for performances of his music. In 1891, he went to America where he was invited to conduct the New York Symphony at the opening of Carnegie Hall.

He died in St. Petersburg on November 6, 1893. The cause of his death was officially declared as cholera; an infection usually contracted from drinking dirty or contaminated water.

The Nutcracker

Piotr Ilyich Tchaikovsky's ballet, **The Nutcracker**, written in 1892, is based on a story by German author E.T.A. Hoffmann. The ballet was choreographed by Marius Petipa and Lev Ivanov. A choreographer designs the dances for a ballet.
In The Nutcracker, a Christmas present, a nutcracker, comes to life as a handsome prince. He takes the young girl who received him as a present on some fantastic adventures. This is one of Tchaikovsky's most famous compositions, and perhaps the most popular ballet in the world.

This is a summary of the story of The Nutcracker.

Act I

It is Christmas Eve and Dr. Stahlbaum and his wife, a former ballerina, are giving a party. Their children, Clara and Fritz, are happy to see the guests. All of the children are given toys. The mysterious Dr. Drosselmeyer is at the party, and performs magic tricks for the children. Dr. Drosselmeyer gives Clara a Nutcracker. She is fascinated by it, and she believes that it has magical powers. Fritz breaks the Nutcracker, and it mysteriously fixes itself. The party comes to an end, the guests depart and the family goes to bed.

Clara is restless and cannot sleep. She sneaks downstairs looking for the Nutcracker. At the stroke of midnight, strange things begin to happen. The room fills with giant mice who attack Clara. The Nutcracker, leading an army of life-size toy soldiers, come to Clara's rescue. The Rat King, who is the leader of the mice attacks the Nutcracker, and Clara hits him with her shoe. The Nutcracker wins the battle and is transformed into a handsome prince.

The Nutcracker Prince turns Clara's house into the Land of Snow. The Snow Queen and the Nutcracker Prince dance with the Snowflakes. Clara and the Nutcracker Prince depart for the Kingdom of Sweets in an enchanted sleigh.

Act II

Clara and the Nutcracker Prince travel across the Lemonade Sea to the beautiful Land of Sweets, ruled by the Sugar Plum Fairy. At the Kingdom of Sweets, the cooks are preparing delicious treats for their visit. The Sugar Plum Fairy welcomes them to her kingdom. In Clara's honor, the Sugar Plum Fairy has her subjects dance for them while they eat. After, the Sugar Plum Fairy and the Nutcracker Prince dance a grand pas de deux.

As the celebration concludes, Clara drifts off to sleep. She awakens at home, but it appears all this was just a dream. Christmas Eve is over. Clara, still thinking of the marvelous dream, is sitting at home by the Christmas tree, with the Nutcracker-Doll on her lap.

Waltz of the Flowers and Dance of the Sugar Plum Fairy

The "Waltz of the Flowers" is a piece from the second act of The Nutcracker. This is one of Tchaikovsky's most well-known compositions. It has been performed and arranged for many combinations of instruments and instrumental groups.

The "Dance of the Sugar Plum Fairy" is a dance from Act 2 of the Nutcracker. The Sugar Plum Fairy dances a pas de deux with her prince. A pas de deux is a dance duet in which two dancers, typically a male and a female, perform ballet steps together. This dance was choreographed by Lev Ivanov.

Choreographer Marius Petipa envisioned the Sugar Plum Fairy's music sounding like "drops of water shooting from a fountain." To achieve this, Tchaikovsky used an instrument called a *celesta*. The celesta looks a little like a piano but has metal plates instead of strings. The plates are hit by hammers, producing a soft, bell-like sound. Tchaikovsky wrote, "The celesta is midway between a tiny piano and a Glockenspiel, with a divinely wonderful sound."

The "Dance of the Sugar Plum Fairy" is one of the ballet's best known musical works.

Answer the following questions.

a. Who composed *The Nutcracker*? _____

b. In what country was he born? _____

c. In what era did he live? _____

d. How many symphonies did he write? _____

e. What type of work is *The Nutcracker*? _____

f. Name a dance from *The Nutcracker*. _____

g. Who choreographed *The Nutcracker*?

        1. _____

        2. _____

h. What is a choreographer? _____

_____

i. What unique instrument is featured in *The Nutcracker*? _____

History Level 5

George Frideric Handel (1685 - 1759) Baroque Era

George Frideric Handel was born on February 23, 1685, in Halle Germany. His father, a barber-surgeon, wanted his son to be a lawyer. However, Handel loved music and practiced on a small keyboard instrument called a clavichord, given to him by his aunt.

In 1693, while visiting the royal court, Handel had an opportunity to play the great organ. When the Duke heard him play, he convinced his father to give him musical training. Handel studied with the organist of St. Michel's in Halle. He learned how to compose, and how to play violin and oboe as well as organ and harpsichord.

In 1702, Handel followed his father's suggestion and entered law school at the University of Halle. After his father's death in the following year, he left his law studies and accepted a position as the organist at Halle Cathedral. The following year, he moved to Hamburg and worked as a violinist and harpsichordist at the opera house. It was there that Handel's first operas were written and produced.

In 1710, Handel accepted the position of Kapellmeister to George, Elector of Hanover, who was soon to be King George I of Great Britain. In 1712, he settled in England where George's wife Queen Anne gave him a yearly income.

Handel wrote operas and oratorios plus music for instruments and ensembles. In 1727, he applied for British citizenship and adopted England as his new home. When King George I died, Handel wrote the music for the coronation of the new king. *Zadok the Priest*, one of these compositions, is still performed today at British coronations.

By 1741, Handel had completed the oratorio Messiah. The first performance of Messiah was given in Ireland in 1742 and was a great success. Many people, to this day, stand during the performance of the "Hallelujah Chorus." Some historians disagree, but the legend is that when the king first heard the "Hallelujah Chorus" he rose to his feet, overcome with emotion. Since the king stood, so did the entire audience. The tradition continues to this day of standing when the "Hallelujah Chorus" from Messiah is performed.

Handel died on April 14, 1759. He was given the honor of a state funeral and was buried in Westminster Abby in London, England. More than 3,000 people attended his funeral.

What is an Oratorio?

An *oratorio* is a large composition for orchestra, choir, and soloists based on a religious theme. Some of the components of an oratorio are:

- *overture* - the musical introduction to the oratorio.
- *recitative* - a kind of musical declamation used during the oratorio, sung in the rhythm of ordinary speech often with many words on the same note.
- *aria* - an accompanied song for a solo voice.
- *chorus* - a large group of singers that performs together with an orchestra.

Messiah

Messiah is an oratorio composed in 1741 by George Frideric Handel. The **libretto,** which is the term used for the text of the oratorio, is based on verses from the Old and New Testaments of the Bible.

It is believed that Handel composed Messiah in only three or four weeks in August and September of 1741. What makes this amazing is the scale of this work. The score is 259 pages, and it takes nearly two hours to perform.

The "Hallelujah Chorus" from Messiah

The "Hallelujah Chorus" is part of Handel's Messiah. It is written for a chorus consisting of soprano, alto, tenor and bass with orchestra. The voices in a four part chorus are:

- *soprano* - sung by womens high voices
- *alto* - sung by womens low voices
- *tenor* - sung by mens high voices
- *bass* - sung by mens low voices

The text for "Hallelujah Chorus" comes from the book of Revelation in the New Testament. The word 'Hallelujah' means praise the Lord and is used in worship as an expression of rejoicing.
Text:
> Hallelujah!
> For the Lord God omnipotent reigneth;
> The kingdom of this world is become the kingdom of our Lord and of his Christ;
> and He shall reign for ever and ever.
> King of Kings and Lord of Lords.
> Hallelujah!

The example below is the opening of the chorus from the Hallelujah Chorus. Each voice part of the chorus receives its own staff line.

Hallelujah Chorus uses a technique called **word painting**. Word painting, sometimes called tone painting or text painting, is the technique of writing music that mirrors the actual meaning of a song.

In Hallelujah chorus low notes symbolize the world while the kingdom of the Lord is sung on high notes. The Hallelujah section has a joyful sound characterized by arpeggios and chromatic notes occurring in a major scale. The line *"for ever and ever"* is repeated over and over.

Wolfgang Amadeus Mozart (1756 - 1791) Classical Era

Wolfgang Amadeus Mozart was born in Salzburg, Austria, on January 27, 1756. He was born into a family of musicians and was an incredible child prodigy. Under the strong influence of his father, Mozart began composing music at the age of five! Here is a brief timeline of his life:

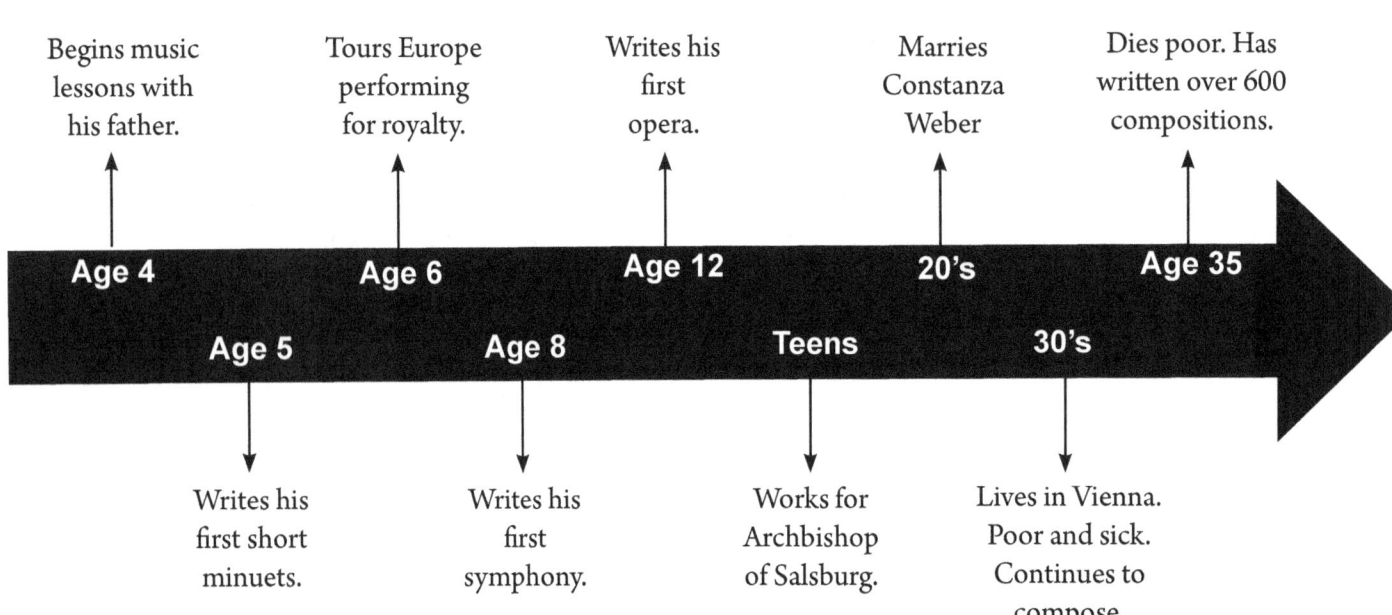

Opera

An *opera* is a play with music. The actual word "opera" is Italian for "work" and was first used in England in 1656. The earliest Italian operas were called favola in musica (fable in music) and drama per musica (drama by means of music).

The construction of an opera is like that of a play. It can be anywhere from one to five acts, and last anywhere from 30 minutes to five hours. The average opera is usually about 3 hours long.
Like plays, operas are staged and use sets and costumes.

Operas usually begin with an *overture*. An overture is a piece of music played by the orchestra that contains melodies from the main part of the opera. The purpose of the overture is to inform the audience that the opera is starting and to set the mood.

Elements of an Opera

Here are some of the elements that are found in an opera:

Recitatives
Recitatives are simple melodies sung at the speed of normal speech. There were originally accompanied by a harpsichord, and in later operas, by the orchestra.

Arias
Arias are songs that can be taken out of an opera and sung as separate musical performances. Most operas are remembered for their finest arias. Arias are often challenging to perform, and give singers the opportunity to show off their voices.

Ensembles
Ensembles occur when characters in the opera sing together. They range from short duets to long, complex pieces involving many characters. Some of Mozart's ensembles can last for 20 minutes!

Choruses
A chorus is a group of singers, singing together. They supply the crowd scenes and extra characters in the opera, as well as the opportunity for beautiful choral music. Members of the chorus may portray servants, party guests, or other unnamed characters.

The Magic Flute (1791)

Mozart's famous opera, **The Magic Flute, Die Zauberflöte** in German, was composed in 1791. The **libretto** or text of the opera was written by Emanuel Schikaneder. It tells a fanciful and extraordinary story that includes a bird seller, a princess, a young prince who wants to rescue her, an evil Queen of the Night, a wise priest, and of course, a magic flute. The story is very complicated, but the music is beautiful and unforgettable.

The Magic Flute is a genre or type of opera called **Singspiel**. Singspiel (pronounced "zing-shpeel") originated in German-speaking countries and found its roots in comic opera. The translation of singspiel is "sing-play." It includes spoken dialogue between the singing, and often, an exotic or fanciful theme.

The Magic Flute is the most famous example of Singspiel. When Mozart was composing, opera was dominated by Italian traditions and language. Mozart decided to write this opera in German as a way to show pride and love of his country and culture and to connect with the common people, not just the elite. It contains a diverse cast of characters and some of Mozart's most magnificent music.

Queen of the Night Aria from "The Magic Flute"

"Der Hölle Rache kocht in meinem Herzen" ("Hell's vengeance boils in my heart"), is an aria sung by the Queen of the Night, in the second act of The Magic Flute. It is often called "The Queen of the Night Aria." In it, the Queen of the Night, who is in a tremendous rage, places a knife into the hand of her daughter Pamina and demands that she assassinate Sarastro, the Queen's rival.

The Queen of the Night is sung by a *coloratura soprano*. Sopranos sing in the highest range of the four voice parts. However, coloratura sopranos are capable of seemingly superhuman feats. In the Queen of the Night aria, the voice is extremely agile, firing out fast paced notes that ascend as high as the 3rd F above middle C. Coloratura soprano roles have existed from Baroque through 20th century opera.

An amazing performance of this aria by the gifted soprano Diana Damrau can be found on YouTube.

The example below is the opening measures of Der Hölle Rache kocht in meinem Herzen. The piano part is the orchestral reduction. The key is in D minor. **Allegro assai** means very fast.

The excerpt below shows the incredible virtuosity employed by the coloratura soprano in this aria.

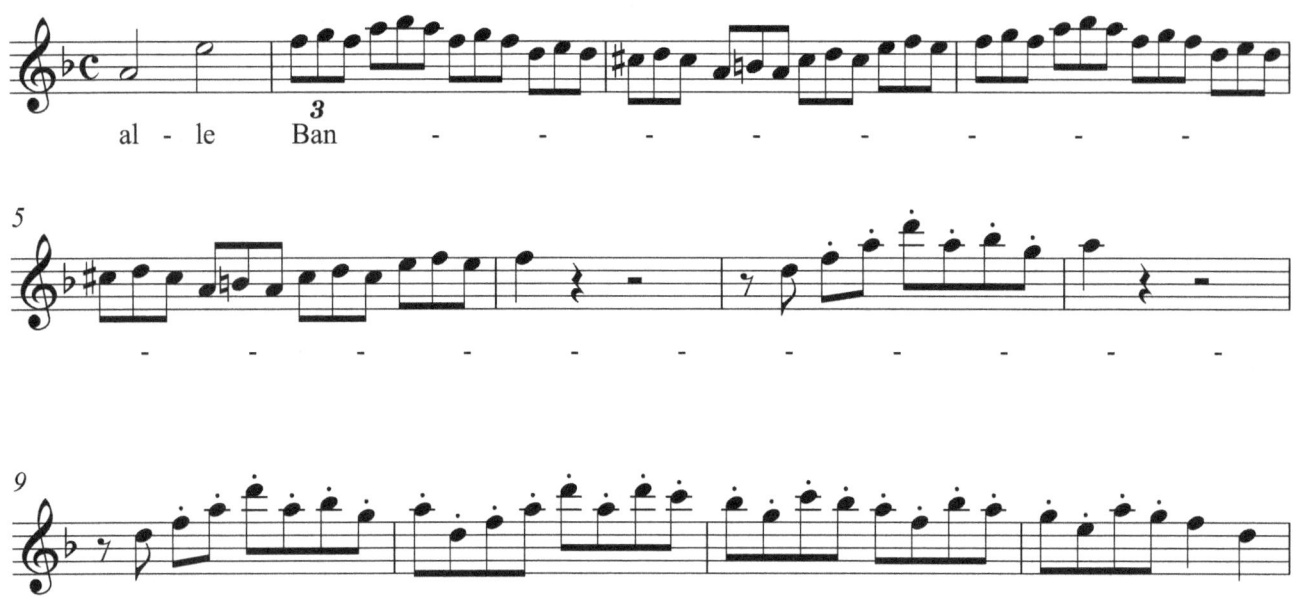

This is the text for Der Hölle Rache kocht in meinem Herzen in German with English translation.

Der Hölle Rache kocht in meinem Herzen,	The vengeance of Hell boils in my heart,
Tod und Verzweiflung flammet um mich her!	Death and despair flame about me!
Fühlt nicht durch dich Sarastro	If Sarastro does not through you feel
Todesschmerzen,	The pain of death,
So bist du meine Tochter nimmermehr.	Then you will be my daughter nevermore.
Verstossen sei auf ewig,	Disowned may you be forever,
Verlassen sei auf ewig,	Abandoned may you be forever,
Zertrümmert sei'n auf ewig	Destroyed be forever
Alle Bande der Natur	All the bonds of nature,
Wenn nicht durch dich!	If not through you
Sarastro wird erblassen!	Sarastro becomes pale! (as death)
Hört, Rachegötter,	Hear, Gods of Revenge,
Hört der Mutter Schwur!	Hear a mother's oath!

Harold Arlen (1905- 1986) Modern Era

Harold Arlen was an American composer, arranger, pianist, and vocalist. He worked as a piano accompanist in vaudeville during his early twenties. His first hit song "Get Happy" was composed with Ted Koehler in 1929.

In the 1930's and 40's, Arlen wrote some of his greatest hits including the score to the movie, The Wizard of Oz. He and his co-writer won the 1939 Academy Award for Best Original Song for "Over the Rainbow."

Stormy Weather, It's Only a Paper Moon, and I've Got the World on a String, are just a few of the standards that live on today and make Harold Arlen one of the most celebrated American composers of the 20th Century.

Over the Rainbow

Harold Arlen composed "Over the Rainbow," with lyricist Edgar Yipsel Harburg, for the 1939 movie The Wizard of Oz.

In the movie, it is sung by actress and singer Judy Garland who plays the role of Dorothy Gale. This film introduced Garland's powerful voice to the public. Visit YouTube for a recording of Garland's performance. Over the Rainbow is written for solo voice and orchestra. It follows a type of song form called AABA song form. This was a standard form used during the first part of the 20th century by composers like Harold Arlen, George Gershwin, and Irving Berlin. AABA songs are usually 32 bars in length and preceded by an Introduction.

AABA song form contains an opening section (A), a bridge (B), and a final A section. It is used in a variety of music genres including pop, jazz, and gospel.

The typical AABA song form follows this outline:

(Introduction)   **A** = 8 bars   **A** = 8 bars   **B** = 8 bars   **A** = 8 bars

AABA has no separate chorus, and the title usually appears at the beginning of each A section. In Over the Rainbow, each A section begins with the lyrics "Somewhere Over the Rainbow." The B section is contrasting and brings the listener back to the last A section.

The lyrics to Over the Rainbow help to illustrate the AABA song structure form.

Introduction	When all the world is a hopeless jumble, and the raindrops tumble all around, heaven opens a magic lane.
	When all the clouds darken up the skyway, There's a rainbow highway to be found, Leading from your window pane.
	To a place behind the sun, Just a step beyond the rain.
A	Somewhere over the rainbow, way up high, There's a land that I dreamed of, Once in a lullabye.
A	Somewhere over the rainbow, skies are blue, And the dreams that you dare to dream, Really do come true.
B	Someday day I'll wish upon a star, and wake up where the clouds are far behind me. Where troubles melt like lemon drops, Away above the chimney tops, That's where you'll find me.
A	Somewhere over the rainbow, skies are blue, And the dreams that you dare to dream, Really do come true. If happy little bluebirds fly. Beyond the rainbow, Why, oh why can't I?

Answer the following questions.

a) Where was Handel born? _____

b) In what music era did Handel live? _____

c) What country did Handel adopt as his new home? _____

d) What is an oratorio? _____

e) When did Handel compose Messiah? _____

f) What voices make up the 4 parts of the chorus in Hallelujah Chorus?

_____   _____   _____   _____

g) What is word painting? _____

_____

h) Give one example of word painting in Hallelujah Chorus. _____

_____

i) What is an opera? _____

j) In what era did Mozart compose? _____

k) What year did Mozart compose "The Magic Flute?" _____

l) What genre or type of opera is "The Magic Flute?" _____

m) What language did Mozart use for "The Magic Flute?" _____

n) What is an aria? _____

_____

o) What type of soprano sings the Queen of the Night aria? _____

Choose the correct answer.

The composer of the Wizard of Oz:

☐ Harold Arlen ☐ George Gershwin ☐ Irving Berlin

Harold Arlen was:

☐ French ☐ Russian ☐ American

"Over the Rainbow" was written for:

☐ Bette Davis ☐ Judy Garland ☐ Beyonce

The song form of "Over the Rainbow" is:

☐ AABA ☐ ABBA ☐ ABAB

History Level 6

The Baroque Era (ca 1600 - 1750)

The word **Baroque** is used to describe a style of art from a specific period in history. *Art* can mean a lot of things. Here, it applies to painting, architecture, and most importantly to our field of study, music.

All Baroque art, architecture, and music was created around 1600 to 1750. However, Baroque music is a style of music. It is not an exact period of time.

What is the Baroque style?

Artists of the Baroque period attempted to evoke emotions in the listener by appealing to their senses. A composer could create a piece of music that would make the listener feel a specific emotion (sadness, happiness, etc.). This was known as **the doctrine of the affections**.

Baroque music is tuneful, very organized, and its melodies are often highly decorated and elaborate. This music can be quite dramatic.

A lot of Baroque music is **contrapuntal** or based on **counterpoint**. This means that there can be many different lines of music (or melodies) all going their own way. These single melodies weave together to make a whole piece of music.

The best way to understand Baroque music, is to listen to the great Baroque composers.

There are many great composers from the Baroque era. The greatest one is Johann Sebastian Bach (1685–1750).

Other famous baroque composers include:

Johann Pachelbel (1653–1706)
Antonio Vivaldi (1678–1741)
George Frideric Handel (1685–1759)

Johann Sebastian Bach (1685 - 1750)

Johann Sebastian Bach was born in Eisenach, Germany, where his father, a musician, taught him to play violin and harpsichord. By the time Johann was 10, both his parents had died. Johann was raised by his older brother who was a church organist. Johann also became a very skilled organist.

Bach's life has three major periods.

The Weimar period. Bach worked for the Duke of Weimar. In this period he became an organ virtuoso and wrote many great works for the instrument.

The Cöthen period. Bach worked for the Prince of Anhalt-Cöthen. During this period he composed a lot of chamber music including suites, instrumental sonatas, and the Brandenburg Concertos.

The Leipzig period. During this period Bach became the cantor, organist, and music composer for St. Thomas Lutheran Church in Leipzig, Germany. Bach remained there for the rest of his life.

Bach wrote music for keyboard instruments (harpsichord, clavichord, organ), orchestra, choirs, chamber groups, and many solo instruments. He is considered one of the greatest musical geniuses in history. In fact, he is such an important composer, that the year of his death (1750), is used to mark the end of the Baroque Era.

Two-part Invention in C major, BWV 772 - J.S. Bach

Bachs *Inventions and Sinfonias,* also known as the *Two and Three-Part Inventions* are a collection of thirty pieces for keyboard. There are 15 two-part and 15 three-part inventions in the masterpiece. Bach said that he composed the Inventions "for amateurs of the keyboard to achieve a cantabile style of playing in two and three parts." They were written as musical teaching pieces for his students.
The two-part inventions were composed in the Cöthen period, and the three-part inventions (Sinfonias)were completed at the beginning of the Leipzig period.

Polyphony is the performance of multiple melodies at the same time. It's a little like two people giving speeches next to each other, but the speeches are different. Imagine having four speakers giving four different speeches at the same time. Eventually, rules developed to control these multiple melodies. These rules became known as counterpoint or the practice of controlling the relationship between the different melodies.

Polyphony is one of the musical textures. Texture is how you hear the music. It may sound dense, thick, thin, or a number of different ways. Polyphony is typically described as thick or densely textured, due to the independence of multiple melodic lines.

An invention is a short composition for a keyboard instrument using two-part **counterpoint**. In a two-part invention, there are two lines of music that interweave with one another. As a result, two part inventions are **polyphonic**.

Inventions use techniques we have covered in past melody writing lessons. These are:

- *motives*: short melodic and rhythmic ideas used to create a melody
- *imitation*: the technique of repeating a musical idea (motive) in another voice or part.
- *sequence*: the repetition of a motive or phrase at a higher or lower pitch.

Below are the opening four measures of J.S. Bach's Two-Part Invention in C major, BWV 772. BWV is a numbering system used to identify Bach's compositions. This invention is based on a seven note motive found in m.1. Imitation of the opening motive can be found in the bass clef in m.1. A sequence moving downward can be found in mm.3 and 4.

Brandenburg Concerto No. 5 - Johann Sebastian Bach

The six Brandenburg Concerti, BWV 1046-1051, by Johann Sebastian Bach is a collection of chamber music works presented to Christian Ludwig, the Margrave of Brandenburg in 1721. Margrave is a title that used to be given to Governors of German provinces.

He assembled these six *concerti grossi* and presented them, as a type of job application, to the Margrave. A **concerto grosso** is a baroque work for orchestra. It usually has three movements and contains a group of solo instruments called the **concertino** that contrasts with the full string orchestra which is known as the **ripieno**.

Bach's title for these works was "concertos for a variety of instruments," since each one uses a different combination of instruments. He tried to use as many different combinations of common instruments as he could. Bach never actually called them the Brandenburg Concertos. The name was given to the pieces by a biographer after his death.

The Fifth Concerto in D major for **violin, flute**, and **harpsichord** makes use of a very popular chamber music ensemble (violin, flute, and harpsichord). These three instruments are the *concertino*. Bach, himself a keyboard virtuoso, included an amazing solo harpsichord cadenza in this concerto.

The first movement of this concerto is in **ritornello** form. In this form, a repeated section of music, known as the ritornello alternates with different musical sections.

Below is the opening of the Brandenburg Concerto No. 5. by J.S. Bach. The score below is an *open score*. In open score, each instrument has its part written on a separate staff. Traditionally the instrument names are written in Italian and appear on the left of the score from highest to lowest. On this score, the top line is the flute, and the bottom is the harpsichord, with the string section between them.

The Classical Era (ca 1750 - 1825)

The Classical era follows the Baroque era. Music from the Classical era was composed around 1750 to 1825.

Classical music is clear, structured and balanced. Form is very important, as well as harmony and tonality—that is, the key in which a piece is written.

Classical music uses dynamic contrast to emphasize movement from the tonic to new keys and then a return to the tonic. It is often loud one moment and then soft the next. It changes volume frequently. It is different from Baroque music in that it is simpler in style, without the heavy figurations and ornamentation. It is not polyphonic, that is, there is no weaving together of different tunes like those found in Baroque music.

Classical music often has a clear tune or melody with an accompaniment. Music with a single line of melody and a harmonic accompaniment is called **homophonic music** or **homophony**.

Most classical music is **absolute music**. This means that it is written specifically for the sake of being music. There are no pictorial or literary associations. It is not supposed to depict or portray anything. It's just beautiful music!

Large forms featured in the Classical period include the solo sonata, symphony, and the concerto. This period also saw a rise in **chamber music**. Chamber music is composed for smaller groups of musicians. These groups consist of two to ten players, with one player on each part. Examples of chamber music include trios, quartets, and quintets.

The greatest composers of the classical period are:

Joseph Haydn (1732–1809).
Wolfgang Amadeus Mozart (1756–1791).
Ludwig van Beethoven (1770–1827).

The classical period ended before Beethoven died. In fact, Beethoven was the one who ended it. Beethoven's later music was so new and unique that it had to be called something completely different.

Sonata Form in the Classical Era

Sonata form reached its zenith in the Classical era at the hands of Haydn, Mozart, and Beethoven.

Sonata form consists of three main sections:

1. **The exposition**: this is the opening section of sonata form. In this section, the composer introduces themes or melodies. Often there are two contrasting themes in two contrasting keys. Contrasting key or tonality is an essential part of this form.
2. **The development**: this is the middle section, and the composer *develops* the themes stated in the exposition. This developing is often done through movement to different keys.
3. **The recapitulation**: in this section the composer returns to the main themes stated in the exposition. This section does not usually change key and remains in the tonic throughout.

Sonata form was used as the basis for movements of solo sonatas, symphonies, concertos and chamber music.

Eine Kleine Nachtmusik (1st Mvt.) Wolfgang Amadeus Mozart

Wolfgang Amadeus Mozart (1756 - 1791) was one of the most important composers of the Classical era. He composed over 600 works, including some of the worlds most famous symphonies, chamber music, operas, and choral music.

Mozart gave the name **Eine kleine Nachtmusik** to his Serenade No. 13 for strings in G major, K 525. It is one of his most popular pieces, and the opening theme is famous. It was composed in 1787.

The title Eine kleine Nachtmusik means: "A little Night Music." "Nachtmusik" was a title that was given to serenades in the 18th century.

The genre of this work is chamber music. It is composed for two violins, viola, and cello and optional double bass. It can be performed as a string quartet or by a small group of string instruments, with one added double bass.

The first movement of Eine kleine Nachtmusik is in sonata form.

The complete work consists of 4 movements.

Choose the correct answers.

a. The Baroque period occurred approximately:	☐	1600-1700	☐	1650-1725
	☐	2010-2015	☐	1600-1750

b. The following are famous Baroque composers:	☐	J.S. Bach	☐	Vivaldi
	☐	Mozart	☐	Handel

c. These elements can be used to describe Baroque music:	☐	counterpoint	☐	doctrine of affections
	☐	romantic	☐	highly ornamented

d. These are Bach's 3 main periods.	☐	Leipzig	☐	Weimar
	☐	Berlin	☐	Cöthen

e. Bach composed for the following mediums.	☐	keyboard	☐	orchestra
	☐	choir	☐	chamber music

f. How many 2 part inventions did J.S. Bach write?	☐	21	☐	15
	☐	12	☐	6

g. The 3-part inventions are also known as:	☐	sonatas	☐	sinfonias
	☐	dances	☐	fugues

h. The 2-part inventions are written for this many voices:	☐	2	☐	3
	☐	6	☐	32

i. 3 elements found in the 2-part inventions are:	☐	motives	☐	sequence
	☐	imitation	☐	monophony

j. This is the numbering system used to identify Bach's works:	☐	NRA	☐	BWV
	☐	BVW	☐	BMW

Answer the following questions.

a. Who composed Brandenburg Concerto No. 5? _____

b. What genre is this work? _____

c. What 3 instruments are featured in this work? _____

d. What is this group of instruments called? _____

e. The full string orchestra in a concerto grosso is called a

☐ ripieno ☐ concertino ☐ oratorio ☐ sequence

f. The form of the first movement of Brandenburg Concerto No. 5 is

☐ rondo ☐ ritornello ☐ sonata ☐ binary

Answer the following questions as true (T) or false (F).

a. The classical period occured around 1750 to 1825. _____

b. The 3 major composers of the classical period are Haydn, Mozart and Bach. _____

c. Music with a single melodic line and accompaniment is *homophonic*. _____

d. Most classical music is *program music*. _____

e. Sonata form consists of 3 main sections. _____

f. These sections are: the *exhibition*, the *development* and the *recapitulation*. _____

g. Eine kleine Nachtmusik is *chamber music*. _____

h. Eine kleine Nachtmusisk is written for strings. _____

i. Eine kleine Nachtmusik contains 5 movements. _____

j. The first movement of Eine kleine Nachtmusik is in *sonata form*. _____

History Level 7

The Romantic Era (ca 1825 - 1900)

The **Romantic era** comes after the Classical era. This period covers most of the 19th century, from about the years 1825 to 1900.

Romanticism was a cultural movement that started in Europe. This movement influenced philosophical thinking, literature, music, and art.

Romantic music was influenced by the literature and painting of the era. It was marked with deep emotional expression. Romantic music expressed strong feelings through music. It was more pictorial than earlier music and often attempted to describe something, perhaps a scene in nature, a poem, a story, or a particular feeling. Music that has a literary or pictorial association is called **program music**. Pieces were often given descriptive titles like Album Leaf, Nocturne, Impromptu, Humoresque, Intermezzo, Arabesque, Papillons.

A few of the composers from this period include Franz Schubert, Frédéric Chopin, Franz Liszt, Robert Schumann, Johannes Brahms, Felix Mendelssohn, Edvard Grieg, Piotr Ilyich Tchaikovsky, Guisseppe Verdi, Georges Bizet, and many more.

Felix Mendelssohn (1809 - 1847)

Felix Mendelssohn was born in 1809 in Hamburg, Germany to a wealthy family with parents who encouraged him to be a musician.

Mendelssohn was the most celebrated child prodigy since Mozart. He began taking piano lessons from his mother when he was 6 and made his first public concert appearance at the age of 9. As a child, he composed extensively, writing five short operas and 11 symphonies by the time he was in his teens.

Mendelssohn came from a musical family. His sister Fanny was also an excellent pianist and composer. The two of them put on Shakespeare's comedy A Midsummer Night's Dream to entertain family and friends and played all of the characters. Mendelssohn's music for A Midsummer Night's Dream describes the plot and many characters in the play.

Mendelssohn's grandfather was the Jewish philosopher Moses Mendelssohn. Being Jewish in Germany was difficult for the Mendelssohn family. They lived at a time when there were specific taxes and laws that only applied to Jews. Because of this discrimination against Jewish people, (known as anti-Semitism), Mendelssohn's father decided to convert to Christianity and changed the family name to Mendelssohn-Bartholdy.

Mendelssohn can be given credit for reviving the music of Johann Sebastian Bach which was largely forgotten by the 19th century. In 1829 he conducted a performance of Bach's St. Matthew Passion, a work for orchestra, choir and soloists. The concert was so successful it started a renewed and lasting appreciation for the music of Bach.

Mendelssohn traveled extensively. His trips to other countries inspired some of his best music. The Italian and Scottish symphonies were inspired by his travels and are two examples of *exoticism*. Exoticism is a term used to describe music that evokes the atmosphere of far-off lands or cultures. Mendelssohn, a German, wrote symphonies inspired by lands that were not part of his heritage.

Mendelssohn died in 1847 at the age of 38 after suffering from ill health. His life was short. However, he managed to distinguish himself as one of the greatest composers of the Romantic period.

Overture to a Midsummer Nights Dream

A German translation of the Shakespeare play " A Midsummer Nights Dream" became part of the Mendelssohn's library in 1826. Felix loved it and wrote this overture in 1827 when he was just 17 years old.

The genre of this composition is ***concert overture***. A concert overture is a single movement concert piece for symphony orchestra based on a literary idea. Overture to a Midsummer Nights Dream is written for two flutes, two oboes, two clarinets, two bassoons, two horns, two trumpets, ophicleide, timpani, and strings. An ophicleide is a bass brass instrument with keys that was eventually replaced by the tuba.

A concert overture is considered ***program music***. Program music is music that has a literary or pictorial association. It has an extra-musical meaning and evokes images or ideas.

A Midsummer Nights Dream is based on the Shakespeare play of the same name. It involves fairies, love potions, and some very bizarre ideas. The play ends by telling the audience it was nothing but a dream.

A concert overture is a romantic piece, but Mendelssohn uses a few classical elements like sonata form. Sonata form consists of three sections:

1. **The Exposition**. In this section, the composer introduces themes that will be used throughout the composition. There are usually two contrasting themes, and this section ends in a new key (the dominant or relative major).

2. **The Development.** In this section, the composer develops the themes from the exposition. This may be done by exploring motives and sequences based on the themes, but the main feature of the development is the exploration of different keys.

3. **The Recapitulation.** Here, the themes from the exposition return in the tonic key. This section remains in the tonic key and often ends with a ***coda***. Coda means "tail" in Italian. A coda is a concluding section of a piece of music. Its length can vary, but it adds a final embellishment to the end of a composition.

Mendelssohn's overture is in the key of E major, and it begins with an introduction before the exposition starts. This consists of four magical chords that give you the impression that you are in a dream. These chords are played by the wind instruments. They invite the listener to a magical forest near Athens where the play is set.

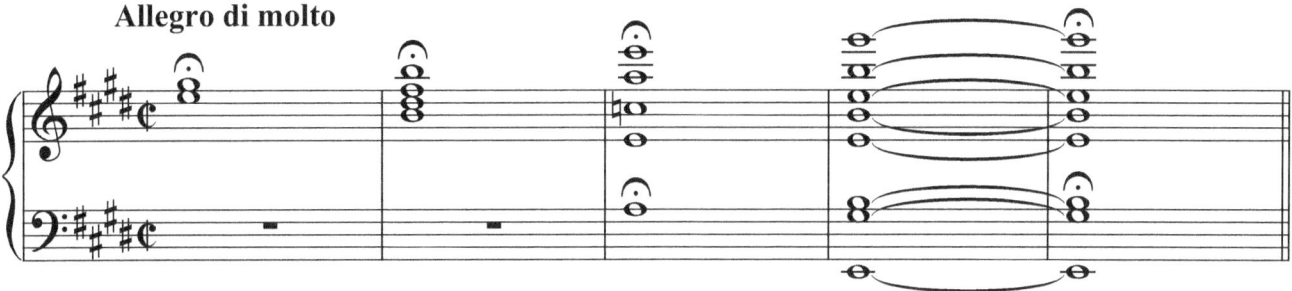

The example below contains the first theme in the exposition. This theme is played by the violins and depicts the fairies scurrying through the woods. It is written in the tonic minor, E minor.

A fanfare-like transition leads to the second theme. The first part shown below is played by the full orchestra and portrays the lovers. The second part shown in Figure 7.4 paints a musical picture of the character named Bottom after Puck's magic has turned him into a donkey. His "hee-hawing" is played by the strings.

Figure 7.4

The exposition is followed by the development section and the recapitulation. The overture ends with the same four magical chords with which it started. Mendelssohn starts the piece like a dream and completes it in the same way, interpreting Shakespeare's play perfectly.

Frédéric Chopin (1810 - 1849)

Frédéric Chopin was born on March 1, 1810, in Żelazowa Wola, Poland. His father was French, and his mother was Polish. His mother introduced him to the piano. He started his musical education at 6, composed his first work at 7, and made his first appearance on stage at 8 years of age. Chopin was devoted to the piano and composed almost exclusively for this instrument.

When Chopin was 20, he left Poland for France and lived the rest of his life in Paris. However, his love and devotion for Poland never died. He carried a small silver box filled with Polish earth when he left Poland. This box was buried with him when he died in Paris in 1849. His heart was put in an urn and placed in the Church of the Holy Cross in Warsaw, Poland.

Chopin's music is infused with his love and devotion to Poland. Some of this influence can be seen in his piano works. He wrote mazurkas and polonaises, based on Polish folk dances.

The majority of his solo pieces are composed in smaller forms and have an improvisatory sound. These include 20 nocturnes, 25 preludes, 17 waltzes, 15 polonaises, 58 mazurkas and 27 etudes. Chopin also wrote larger forms, including the scherzo, the ballade (a genre he invented), and the sonata. The four Ballades and the two Sonatas are among his most significant compositions.

Chopin had a love for opera and the music of opera composer Vincenzo Bellini. Much of his piano music is written in a style called *bel canto*. Bel Canto style translates to "beautiful singing style." Chopin's piano music is noted for its beautiful singing lines and melodies. His music is also known for its virtuosity and its advanced treatment of harmony and rhythm.

Elements in Chopin's Music

Rubato: All of Chopin's music employs rubato. This is an expressive and rhythmic freedom achieved by speeding up and slowing down the tempo of a piece at the discretion of the performer.

Harmony: Unlike composers of the past, Chopin's chords don't just function as a set of tensions and resolutions. Many have a unique, individual, colorful sound. Chopin discovered that dissonance, which creates tension and traditionally requires resolution, can be beautiful by itself. His music often contains chromaticism, unusual modulations, and sudden key changes.

Nationalism: Music based on a composers country is nationalistic. Polish culture, folk songs, and rhythms influence Chopin's music.

Etude Op. 10 No. 12 (Revolutionary)

The term *etude* is used to describe a piece of music that focuses on refining and training a specific aspect of a performers technique. Etudes are sometimes referred to as ***studies***. Many etudes are just repetitions of note patterns and lack real musicality. Chopin's etudes are different. He was the first composer to pioneer the etude as an actual art form. He wrote 27 etudes for piano. Each of the Chopin etudes not only trains a specific technical area but also tells an emotional story. They are anything but repetitive, dry, technical exercises. This musical approach to the etude continued through the Romantic period and other composers, notably Franz Liszt, wrote in this genre.

Chopin's etudes cover many areas of technique, from arpeggios to octaves, but all are designed to develop a legato style of playing.

The Etude in C minor Op. 10, No. 12 is one of Chopin's most recognized compositions. The genre of this etude is ***solo piano piece***. This piece has been given the programmatic title "Revolutionary Etude." It was composed after Chopin heard of Poland's failure in its rebellion against Russia. Chopin never gave titles like this to his compositions, almost always preferring to refer to them by opus and number. He probably did not come up with this title, and actually may have disapproved of it. This nickname might be attributed to an editor or fan of his music.

Most of the technical difficulty in this etude is in the left hand, which has rapid runs, arpeggios, and broken chords. It is in ternary (ABA) form.

A is mm. 1 - 28
B is mm. 29 - 42
A is mm. 43 - 84

The opening eight measures act as in introduction to the main theme which begins in m. 10.

Find and listen to a recording of this etude on the internet.

The Modern Era (ca 1900 - present day)

In the Modern Era (1900 - present), composers followed traditional musical ideas but used their own creative approach. This resulted in freedom in all areas, including melody, rhythm, and chord progression. The development of audio recording technology, computers, and the internet was also very important to the development of modern music.

Music from the Modern era has a lot of variety. There are a number of different "schools" of composition. Many composers had their own way of thinking about composition, and how to compose in new and different ways. These new ways created new genres (types of music) that have names ending in "ism." Examples of these are impressionism, serialism, neoclassicism, expressionism, minimalism, and post-modernism. The Modern period also includes jazz, world music (music from non-European cultures), and electronic music.

Igor Stravinsky (1882 - 1971)

Igor Stravinsky was born in Oranienbaum, Russia. His father was an opera singer and his mother a pianist. Stravinsky began taking piano lessons at age 9. After high school, his parents convinced him to study law. One of his fellow law students was the son of the famous Russian composer Nikolai Rimsky-Korsakov. This connection allowed Stravinsky to take music composition lessons from the great composer.

Stravinsky became famous in the early 1900s when he wrote music for the Russian Ballet, including *The Firebird, Petrushka*, and *The Rite of Spring*. He fled Russia with the outbreak of World War I and took his family to Switzerland. He missed Russia during this period, and he composed music based on Russian Folklore as well as music influenced by jazz.

In 1920 Stravinsky moved his family to Paris where he lived for 20 years. Following the deaths of his wife and a daughter from tuberculosis, in 1939, he moved to the United States and became an American citizen. He died in New York City in 1971, having written more than 100 works.

Petrushka

Petrushka is a ***ballet*** by Igor Stravinsky. Ballet is an art form that consists of music, dancing, and scenery to convey a story or theme. Petrushka is composed for an orchestra with a large percussion section including a piano.

Until 1920, Stravinsky's works were deeply connected to his Russian heritage. The most famous ballet to build upon this Russian pride is Petrushka, composed in 1911. In this ballet, Stravinsky incorporated themes from Russian folk songs.

Petrushka was first performed in 1911 in Paris by the Ballets Russes. The story is based on traditional Russian folklore and features a puppet named Petrushka. Stravinsky's version of the story involves three puppets brought to life by a magician: Petrushka, a Ballerina, and the Moor. Petrushka, a wild and rebellious jester, falls in love with the Ballerina, but she only has eyes for the handsome, arrogant Moor. The Moor kills Petrushka in a duel, but Petrushka's ghost reappears to haunt the magician who brought him to life.

Petrushka is a complicated work that does not follow the conventional rules of tonality. Harmonically and rhythmically it moves away from traditional compositional rules by using unusual scales, polychords, and polyrhythms.

Petrushka has a pitch center (C), but it does not use the conventional pitch relationships that are seen in the major and minor tonal system. Instead, Stravinsky uses the octatonic scale as a basis for this work. An octatonic scale is based on alternating whole steps and half steps. In this case: C, C#, D#, E, F#, G, A, A#, C.

Stravinsky uses ***polyrhythms*** in Petrushka. Polyrhythm involves using two or more differing rhythms at the same time. For example, one musical line may be playing in 3/4 time, while another line is playing in 4/4 time.

Polytonality is also a feature of Petrushka. A polychord is a single chord made up of two or more different chords played at the same time. For example, if you take a C major chord and a D major chord and stack one on top of the other:

C major: C E G
D major: D F# A

The result is a chord that looks like the chord below.

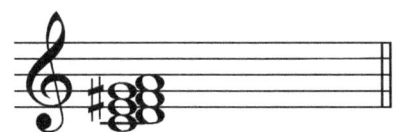

Petrushka does not have the traditional tonic/dominant relationship found in tonal music. A traditional piece of music in C might feature a lot of movement from C (the tonic) to G (the dominant). This tonal relationship is very consonant (pleasing). Stravinsky replaces the dominant chord with a chord based on the augmented fourth. The interval from C to F# is an augmented fourth, and this relationship is very dissonant (displeasing).

Petrushka moves between the two chords: C major (C, E, G) and F# major (F#, A#, C#). The juxtaposition of these two chords represents Petrushka's bold and brash character. There are times when they meet, creating the polychord C, C#, E, F#, G, A# shown below in a. Since it is used so much in the music, this chord has come to be known as the "Petrushka chord." Example b. shows how this chord is derived from notes of the octatonic scale.

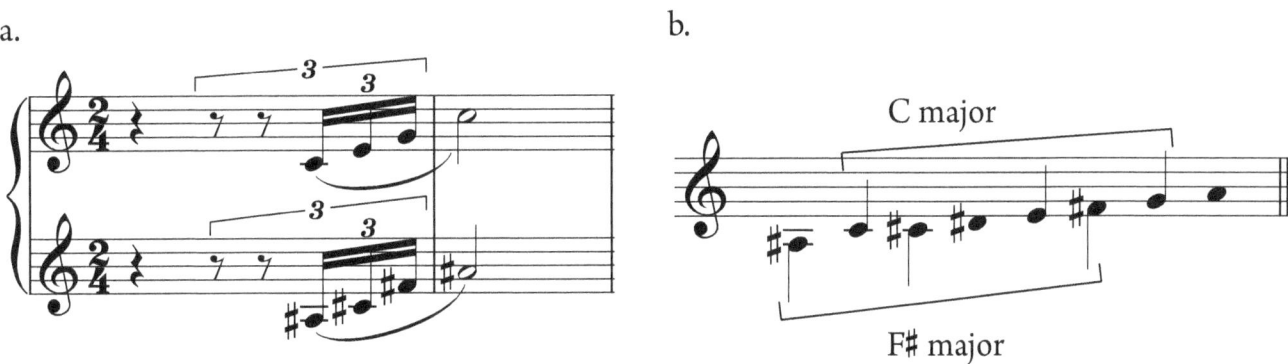

Rondo Form

Form in music is the way a composition is organized. The form is determined by several factors, including changes of key, when new musical material occurs, and when former musical material is restated.

Petrushka is in **rondo form**. In rondo form, musical material stated at the beginning of the piece keeps returning. This opening music can be called the **theme** or the **refrain**. Between statements of the theme or refrain, there are **episodes**. An episode is musical material that is different from the theme.

The theme, or refrain, of a rondo, is the first main melody or musical material that occurs in the piece. It will establish the key of the piece, and the theme will most often be played in this same key. Since it is the first material we hear in the piece, we label this part of the music the A-section.

The episodes usually differ in melody, in musical character, or in key from the theme. We label the first episode the B-section. For each different episode that occurs in the music, we use a different label, such as 'C,' 'D,' and so on.

In rondo form, the theme or A section will keep returning after every episode. One example of rondo form would be ABACA. The theme, or A-section, will always return after every episode.

The length of a Rondo varies depending on the number of sections it contains. ABACA and ABABA are examples of 5 part Rondo forms because they have a total of five sections. ABACABA and ABACADA are examples of 7 part Rondo forms.

Petrushka is a 7 part Rondo with its structure being ABACABA.

Duke Ellington (1899 - 1974)

Edward Kennedy "Duke" Ellington was born in Washington, D.C. on April 29, 1899. He was an American pianist, bandleader, and composer, most often known for his work with big band swing music. Ellington was a talented pianist but is famous for his big bands. These were orchestra-sized jazz bands that played dance music.

As an African-American composer working in Harlem, Ellington was an important part of the Harlem Renaissance, a period of artistic and intellectual production that took place in Harlem, New York in the 1920s. The greatest jazz players in history turned up to play with Ellington, and he wrote music to showcase their talents.

Throughout his life, Duke Ellington helped make jazz music successful throughout the world. He thought the term 'jazz' was not appropriate for his music because it was limiting. He referred to his music as 'American music.'

By the time of his death in 1974, he had composed thousands of original pieces of music including "It Don't Mean a Thing if It Ain't Got That Swing," "Sophisticated Lady," "Mood Indigo," "Solitude," and "Satin Doll."

To this day, Ellington is one of the most prolific composers and has personally contributed more to jazz music than any other person in history.

Jazz

Jazz is a music genre that has its origins in African American communities in the late 19th and early 20th centuries. Major features of jazz are improvisation and rhythm. Jazz musicians express themselves through ***improvisation***, requiring them to be inventive and create music on the spot. They do this by embellishing the melody or by changing melodies rhythmically. A key element of jazz is ***rhythmic syncopation***, which is when accents occur on the off-beat. Some jazz is ***polyrhythmic***, which is when multiple, contrasting rhythms occur at the same time.

Blues

Blues is a musical form started in the United States at the beginning of the 20th century. The blues are derived from spirituals, work songs, and field-hollers by African slaves. The first blues songs originated near the Mississippi River and were called the Delta blues. As African Americans moved throughout the United States, they took the blues with them and developed regional styles of this genre. Blues are the foundation of almost every American musical form in the 20th century, including jazz, rock and roll, hip-hop, and rap.

Twelve-bar Blues

12-bar blues progressions are organized into three 4-bar sections: four bars of the I chord, two bars each of the IV and I chords, and one bar of V, one bar of IV, and two bars of I (or one bar of I and one bar of V).

The piece below is the 12-bar blues in C. The right hand is based on the C blues scale.

Koko

Duke Ellington wrote *Koko* in 1940. This piece is inspired by drumming from African religious ceremonies Ellington heard in New Orleans. He wrote it for his big band which consisted of piano, drums, guitar, trumpets, trombones, clarinets, and saxophones. Koko's genre is ***12 bar blues***.

Koko is divided into an Introduction, seven sections called choruses, and a coda. In jazz music, a chorus is one full statement of a song's form played through. In this case, each chorus contains the complete 12-bar blues progression. Koko is written in the key of E♭ minor, and all the choruses are in 12-bar blues form. Each chorus features different soloists and instrument combinations.

Listen to a recording of Koko on the internet, preferably a recording by Duke Ellington and his Big Band.

Musique Concréte

Musique Concrète was developed in the 1940s by French composer Pierre Schaeffer. It involves composing music based on recorded sounds. Musique concrète uses recordings of natural sounds, like water drips, the human voice, or musical instruments to create aural compositions. The sounds selected and recorded may be modified in various ways. They may be shortened or lengthened, played backwards, or varied in pitch and intensity. The completed work combines all of the sounds into one united composition.

Hugh Le Caine (1914 - 1977)

Hugh Le Caine (1914 -1977) was a Canadian composer and scientist. He received a science degree from Queen's University and worked for the National Research Council of Canada in atomic physics and developing radar systems.

He also focused on electronic music and sound generation and established a studio where he designed electronic instruments. He is considered a pioneer of electronic music.

Dripsody

Dripsody, is an electronic composition, and its genre is **electronic music**. It is an example of musique concrète, and was composed in 1955 by Hugh Le Caine. All of the sounds in this work are derived from the splash of a single drop of water. Le Caine used an eye dropper and recorded the sound of water drops falling into a metal wastebasket for 30 minutes before choosing the sound of one drop on which to base this work. The sound of this drop repeated over and over is heard throughout the work. He manipulated this sound in various ways:

1. He changed the tape speed. Speeding up or slowing down the tape created different pitches. In this way, he was able to assemble some of these pitches into a pentatonic scale.
2. He reversed the tape, playing the sounds backward.
3. He used four different tape loops or recordings of the water to produce repeated patterns or ostinatos.
4. He used tape delay. This was done by playing the sound and re-recording it at the same time creating an echo effect.

The piece begins with a single drop of water and increases in intensity by becoming more rhythmically active and dense until it climaxes in the middle. Then it gradually decreases in intensity and ends where it started, with a single drop of water.

Find a recording of Dripsody on the internet and listen for all of the features listed above.

a) When did the Romantic era occur? _____

b) Music that has a literary or pictorial association is called _____

c) Name two Romantic period composers _____

d) Where was Felix Mendelssohn born? _____

e) Whose music did Mendelssohn help revive? _____

f) What genre is Overture to a Midsummer Nights Dream? _____

g) What author wrote the play that this work is based upon? _____

h) What is the form of Overture to a Midsummer Nights Dream? _____

i) Name the three main sections in this form:

_____   _____   _____

Answer true (T) or false (F) to the following statements.

a. Frédéric Chopin was born in France. _____
b. Chopin composed in the classical era. _____
c. Chopin composed mainly for the piano. _____
d. Chopin wrote in 'bel canto style.' _____
e. 'Nationalism' refers to music with a pictorial or literary association. _____
f. 'Rubato' refers to music from Poland. _____
g. 'Etudes' are sometimes referred to as studies. _____
h. Chopin's Revolutionary Etude is in C minor. _____

Name the composer and genre of the following works:

Petrushka

Composer: _____ Genre: _____

Koko

Composer: _____ Genre: _____

Dripsody

Composer: _____ Genre: _____

Etude Op. 10, No. 12 'Revolutionary'

Composer: _____ Genre: _____

Overture to a Midsummer Nights Dream

Composer: _____ Genre: _____

Name the composer and musical period for the following compositions.

Composition	Composer	Musical Era
Dripsody		
Revolutionary Etude		
Koko		
Overture to a Midsummer Nights Dream		
Petrushka		

History Level 8

The Medieval Era (500- 1450)

The medieval era took place from approximately 500 to 1450 A.D. This was a period of heavy church influence. Music was around before this time and had various developments, but during the medieval era, the use and creation of music was regulated by the church.

The church was the main patron of the arts, including music. Many musicians were trained in the church, and the church had the financial means to buy extravagant items like paper, where eventually music was written down. Our current system of music notation is even rooted in the developments made in the medieval church!

Medieval church music had very specific rules, which included the chanting of prayers. Chanting of this period is called ***plainchant*** and is sometimes referred to as Gregorian chant since Pope Gregory standardized chant for the liturgy. Plainchant is a single line of modal melody, without a measured rhythm, sung in Latin. Modal refers to ancient scales called ***modes***, which were studied in Lesson 3.

Plainchant is ***monophonic***, meaning it is one melody without harmony, resulting in just one musical part. ***Monophony*** is a single melody without accompaniment. Monks would sing the prayer together in unison.

Around the year 900, some simple harmony involving two vocal parts was allowed. This type of simple two-part medieval harmony is called ***organum***. The harmony was made in one of two ways:

- Sometimes a drone, or low, continuous note, was sung while the main melody was sung at the same time. Drones are still used in bagpipe music today.
- Other times, the words of the song would be sung on two different pitches at the same time.

Ordo Virtutum - Hildegard von Bingen

One of the greatest composers of the medieval era was **Hildegard von Bingen**. Hildegard lived from approximately 1098 to 1179. She was a German nun, mystic, poet, and composer who was known for her visions and prophecies. Hildegard wrote poems about her visions and prophecies and set them to music.

Her music is incredibly melodic for the middle ages. The church had very stringent rules about music, yet she was able to incorporate new and extended musical techniques that still fit under the guidelines of the church. She used a wide range of pitches and leaps that were uncharacteristic for the time. These methods were used to give meaning and musical emphasis to the words she wrote.

Hildegard's most renowned work is a musical play called **Ordo Virtutum**. Ordo Virtutum (The Play of the Virtues), composed about 1151, is a liturgical drama, known as a **morality play**. A morality play is a drama designed to teach a moral or lesson. Ordo Virtutum is about the struggle for a human soul between the Virtues and the Devil. The text of this work is in Latin, the language of the Roman Empire, and the official language of the church.

Ordo Virtutum contains 82 different monophonic melodies. All parts are sung in plainchant by women, except that of the Devil. Several notes are sung to each syllable of text. A technique called **melisma**, which consists of many notes sung to one syllable, is used to emphasize important words. Hildegard based the music on modes, which serve to elicit varied feelings, like withdrawal, happiness, sadness, or serenity. The rhythm is free, with no time signatures or meter. The characters in Ordo Virtutum are:

- The Soul, Anima, sung by a female voice.
- The Virtues (Humility, Hope, Chastity, Innocence, Contempt of the World, Celestial Love, Discipline, Modesty, Mercy, Victory, Discretion, Patience, Knowledge of God, Charity, Fear of God, Obedience, and Faith), sung by 17 solo female voices.
- The chorus of the Prophets and Patriarchs, sung by women.
- The chorus of Souls, sung by women.
- The Devil (a male voice) does not sing, he only yells or grunts. According to Hildegard, the Devil cannot produce divine harmony.

Secular Music in the Medieval Era

By the late medieval era, **secular**, or non-religious music, was becoming extremely popular. Secular music employed some of the developments that were made within the church. Royalty also played a prominent part in musical life, since wealthy people could afford to train musicians and pay composers to write for them.

Minstrels and **troubadours** were two types of musicians that were part of Royal court life. Minstrels were not as refined as troubadours and entertained in other ways, like juggling. Troubadours sang songs of chivalry, courtly love, and travel to faraway lands. Secular songs developed more and more during this period using multiple voices and instruments.

Sumer is Icumen In

Sumer Is Icumen In is a medieval English vocal work composed in the mid-13th century. This piece is a **rota**. Rota is another word for a round or canon. A round consists of at least two voices that sing the same melody with each voice beginning at different times.

The text of Sumer Is Icumen In is in Middle English, and the title translates to 'Summer is Coming.' The composer is unknown. This is a **polyphonic** composition for six voices. **Polyphony** consists of two or more melodies singing together. In this case, it's six!

Sumer Is Icumen In contains a repeated two-part section called a **pes** (foot). A pes is a melodic or rhythmic pattern that repeats over and over. A pes is also known as an **ostinato**. Below is the four measure pes or ostinato written in modern notation. It is usually sung by two tenors.

The complete melody of Sumer Is Icumen In is shown below. Rather than being written in one of the modes, which was common in the middle ages, it is in a major key. In modern notation you may see it written in 6/8 or 12/8 time and in any number of keys. This example is in F major. Find a recording of this piece on the internet.

The Renaissance Era (ca 1450 - 1600)

The Renaissance Era (ca. 1450-1600) brought about great change in both sacred and secular music. For most of the Medieval Era, music was reserved for the Church and the wealthy. Advancements and social changes in the Renaissance Era allowed music to flourish in both sacred and secular genres. Despite the Reformation and the Counter Reformation, there was continuous musical growth happening in both the Catholic and the Protestant Churches.

In the Renaissance, the motet and the Mass were the most common forms of sacred music. However, many forms of secular music were being developed. Secular music included ***madrigals***, which were part songs for several voices, and the rise of both instrumental and dance music.

Josquin Des Prez (ca 1440 - 1521)

Josquin des Prez, from the Renaissance era, became known as one of the greatest composers of the 16th century. He is often just called Josquin. Josquin's date and place of birth are not known, but he was probably born between 1440 and 1450 in France or Belgium. As an adult, he enjoyed a successful musical career in Italy.

Josquin's specialties included the use of overlapping vocals, as found in the canon or round, which is a composition of overlapping vocals in the strictest sense. Using these techniques allowed Josquin to be extremely expressive in the setting of text, while also enriching its meaning. Josquin Des Prez is regarded as one of the leading composers of Renaissance choral music. His compositions are still performed throughout the world today.

El Grillo

"*El Grillo*," or "The Cricket," is a light, fun, **a cappella** piece by Josquin. A cappella refers to vocal music without instrumental accompaniment. El Grillo is considered a ***frottola***. This is a polyphonic vocal work, and an ancestor of the madrigal. Josquin wrote three frottole and El Grillo is his most popular. It is written for four voices. The text is in Italian. The English translation of the lyrics are:

>The cricket is a good singer
>Who can hold a long note
>Of drinking the cricket sings
>The cricket is a good singer
>But he doesn't do what birds do,
>After they've sung a bit,
>They go somewhere else,
>The cricket always stays put
>And when the weather is hottest
>He sings solely for love

Josquin uses **word painting** in this piece. Word painting was common in the Renaissance, as the madrigal became popular. Word painting is when the music matches the meaning of the word. For example, on the line "Who can hold a long note," the word "long" is extended. At one point in the refrain, the voices are meant to mimic the chirp of a cricket.

In portions of El Grillo, Josquin uses **homorhythm**. This is a texture where all parts sing in the same rhythm. This rhythm results in a blocked chordal texture. Homorhythmic texture allows the lyrics to be very clear and easy to understand. The opening measures of El Grillo are shown below.

Global Music - The Javanese Gamelan

In 1899, French composer Claude Debussy, upon hearing a Javanese gamelan orchestra wrote: 'Their conservatory is the rhythm of the sea, the wind among the leaves and the thousand sounds of nature...'. For centuries, Indonesians have developed their gamelan orchestras, making sounds that are other worldly, magical, yet still human all at the same time. Since Debussy, other nations have been fascinated and intrigued by this music, and it has spread throughout the world.

The word '**gamelan**' is derived from the Indonesian word meaning 'hammer.' A gamelan is an Indonesian mallet orchestra native to Bali and Java. The gamelan orchestra is made up of several types of mallet instruments like the **metallophone**, a xylophone-like instrument with metal bars struck by mallets, or keyboard-style instruments struck with mallets or hammers, as well as different drums, flutes, and occasionally stringed instruments or vocalists.

Gamelan instruments are tuned differently than those in Western music. There are two tuning systems that gamelan orchestras use, one which consists of five notes, and one which has seven notes. Many of the same instruments occur in pairs, with each one being tuned slightly differently than the other. When two of the same instruments play a note in unison, the different sound waves vibrate against each other, creating a quality of sound gamelan musicians call *ombak*, or 'shimmering sound.'

Traditional Javanese gamelan music is divided into two parts: a central melody, and a part that embellishes that central melody. Gamelan music is not written down or notated. It is handed down orally (or aurally) from generation to generation.

Search the internet for videos and recordings of Gamelan orchestras.

Indian Music - The Raga

Much of Western music is based on modes, especially the major and minor modes. A *raga* is a mode (scale) found in Indian classical music and used in improvised performances. There are over 300 ragas.

Raga means 'color.' Just as each color in the spectrum is unique, each raga has a unique sound. The sound of each raga is associated with certain emotions, times of day, Hindu deities, and seasons. Ragas often use *microtones*. These are smaller intervals than those found in Western music. The traditional half step may be subdivided into quarter steps or quarter tones.

Indian classical music is improvised, so each performance is different. Despite this, Indian musicians do not play whatever they want. Their improvisations must follow the rules of the raga.

Each raga contains:

- the raga scale, which contains the specific pitches used in the piece.
- the Arohana, an ascending form of the scale.
- the Avarohana, a descending form of the scale, which may not be the same as the Arohana.
- the Vadi, an important note that is played more frequently than other notes.
- the Samvadi, a note of seconday importance.

All of these elements work together to form a larger melody called the *chalan*. When musicians master the chalan, they use it as a basis for their improvisation.

The number of instruments in a raga may vary, but there are at least three instruments involved in a performance: a drone, a drummer, and one or more melody instruments. The melody instrument plays the raga. One of the most common Indian melody instruments is the *sitar*, a long-necked, guitar-like, string instrument with a gourd-shaped resonance chamber.

The main percussion instruments used in North India are called *tabla*, a pair of drums that are tuned to work with the notes of the raga. The drums often introduce a regular rhythmic cycle called a *tala*. Tala means 'clap' and is a rhythmic beat that keeps the time of the raga.

The drone instrument is often a *tanpura*. The tanpura looks like a sitar, but has only four strings and is missing the gourd-like resonance chamber. These strings are tuned to the first and fifth scale notes and are played continuously to act as a reference point for the person playing the melody. This helps the soloist stay on track throughout their improvisation.

Find and listen to examples of Indian Raga music on the internet.

Sitar

Tabla

Tanpura

Music Terms and Signs

Terms

accelerando, accel.	becoming quicker
accent	a stressed note
ad libitum, ad lib.	at the liberty of the performer
adagio	slow
agitato	agitated
alla, all'	in the manner of
allargando	getting slower and broader
allegretto	fairly fast, a little slower than allegro
allegro	fast
andante	moderately slow, at a walking pace
andantino	a little faster than andante
animato	lively, animated
arco	for strings return to bowing after pizzicato or col legno.
attacca	begin immediately, proceed without a break
a tempo	return to the original tempo
ben, bene	well
bewegt	with movement, agitated
calando	becoming slower and softer
cantabile	in a singing style
cédez	yield, slow down
col, coll', colla, colle	with
comodo	at a comfortable tempo
con	with
con brio	with vigor
con espressione	with expression
con fuoco	with fire
con grazia	with grace
con moto	with motion
con sordino	with the use of a mute

crescendo, cresc.	becoming louder
da capo, D.C.	from the beginning
D.C. al fine	repeat from the beginning and end at *Fine*
dal segno, D.S. 𝄋	from the sign
decrescendo, decresc.	becoming softer
diminuendo, dim.	becoming softer
dolce	sweetly, gentle
dolente	sad
e, ed	and
espressivio, espress.	expressive, with expression
fine	the end
forte, f	loud
fortissimo, ff	very loud
fortepiano, fp	loud, then suddenly soft
giocoso	humorous, joyful
grandioso	grand, play in a grand and noble style
grazioso	gracefully
grave	slow and solemn
langsam	slowly
largamente	broadly
larghetto	fairly slow, not as slow as largo
largo	very slow
léger	lightly
leggiero	light
lentement	slowly
lento	slow
l'istesso tempo	at the same tempo
loco	return to the normal register
ma	but
maestoso	majestically
mano destra, m.d.	right hand

mano sinistra, m.s.	left hand
marcato	play marked or stressed
martellato	strongly accented, hammered
mässig	moderately
meno	less
meno mosso	less motion
mesto	sad, mournful
mezzo forte, mf	moderately loud
mezzo piano, mp	moderately soft
mit Ausdruck	with expression
moderato	at a moderate tempo
modéré	at a moderate tempo
molto	much, very
morendo	dying, fading away
mouvement	movement, tempo, motion
non	not
ottava, 8va	the interval of an octave
pesante	heavy, play with weight
pedale, ped	pedal
pianissimo, pp	very soft
piano, p	soft
piu	more
piu mosso	more motion
pizzicato	pluck the strings, for string instruments
poco	little
poco a poco	little by little
prestissimo	as fast as possible
presto	very fast
primo, prima	first, the upper part of a duet
quasi	almost, as if
quindicesima alta, 15ma	play 2 octaves higher

rallentando, rall.	slowing down
risoluto	resolute, bold, strong
ritardando, rit.	slowing down gradually
ritenuto, riten	suddenly slower
rubato	flexible tempo with slight variations of speed to enhance musical expression.
scherzando	playful, play in a light-hearted happy manner
schnell	fast
sehr	very
secondo, seconda	second, lower part of a duet
semplice	simple
sempre	always
senza	without
sforzando, sf, sfz	sudden strong accent on a single note or chord
simile	continue in the same manner as has just been indicated
sonore	sonorous, resonant; with rich tone
sopra	above, indicates piano player crossing hands
sostentuto	sustained, play in a prolonged manner
staccato	play short and detached
stringendo	gradually faster, pressing forward
subito	suddenly
tacet	be silent, voice or instrument does not play or sing
tempo	speed at which music is performed
Tempo Primo, Tempo I	return to the original tempo
tranquillo	tranquil, quiet
tre corde	3 strings, release the left pedal on the piano
troppo	too much
tutti	a passage for the whole ensemble
una corda	1 string, depress the left pedal on the piano
vite	fast

vivace   lively, brisk

vivo   lively

volta   time, *prima volta*=1st time, *seconda volta*=2nd time

volti subito, v.s.   turn the page quickly

Signs

 **accent** - a stressed note

 common time - symbol for 4/4

 **crescendo** - becoming louder

 **decrescendo** - becoming softer

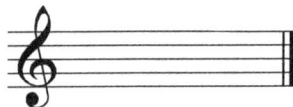 **double bar line** - the end of a piece

 **fermata** - hold note or rest longer than written value

 **glissando, gliss** - a continuous sliding up or down from one pitch to another

 **slur** - play the notes smoothly (legato)

staccato - play short and detached

 **tie** - hold for the combined value of the tied notes

repeat marks - at the second sign go back to the first sign and repeat the music from there. The first sign is left out if the music is repeated from the beginning.

pedal symbol - press/release the right pedal.

tenuto mark - when placed over or under a note, hold it for its full value.

dal segno, D.S. - from the sign.

8va - play one octave higher than written pitch.

8va - play one octave lower than written pitch.

down bow - on a string instrument, play the note by drawing the bow downward.

up bow - on a string instrument, play the note by drawing the bow upward.

breath mark - take a breath or a small break

www.ingramcontent.com/pod-product-compliance
Lightning Source LLC
Chambersburg PA
CBHW081625100526
44590CB00021B/3609